What Leaders Are Saying

"Nobody 'gets' prayer evangelism better than Alvin Vander Griend. He has taken literally decades of experience and put it together in a practical and readable book. In a very real way, this is simply the New Testament lifestyle put into today's culture that releases the love of Christ and draws people to Jesus."

Dave Butts
Chairman, *National Prayer Committee*

"The prayer-care-share lifestyle is strongly biblical, practical and indescribably fulfilling. It is available to every follower of Jesus. Alvin Vander Griend has been one of the pioneers and leaders in introducing this wonderful lifestyle to tens of thousands of Christ followers. This may be the best of all of his writings. I highly commend it to you."

Paul Cedar
Mission America Coalition

"I am delighted to see this book in print. It will not only mean that many more people will be around the throne because they have been loved into heaven, it will also assist followers of Christ to fulfill His last command. I am convinced that contained in the three little words 'prayer-care-share' are all the biblical responsibilities believers have toward non-believers. Those who follow the simple steps Vander Griend lays out will be closer to fulfilling those responsibilities."

Dennis Fuqua
Director, *International Renewal Ministries*

"Fantastic, Alvin! You've done it again. This book is yet another important resource for those who live, and equip others to live, a prayer-care-share lifestyle. You include all the vital components. Love, which must motivate our praying, permeate our caring, and activate our sharing. Ministry Teams, which have been ignored until now—most Christ-followers who are fearful of evangelism, will readily pray, serve, and witness when teamed with others.

Aftercare recognizes that evangelism must continue into disciple-making and that effective disciple-making produces faith sharing. This customizable course is biblical, understandable, and offers practical action steps. I believe this tool will serve the LOVE2020.com movement well. Our thanks for your long obedience in the prayer-care-share direction (with homage to Eugene Peterson). You are truly a pioneer who continues to bring fresh thought to the movement."

Phil Miglioratti
National Pastors' Prayer Network
http://Pray.Network

LOVING PEOPLE TO JESUS

PRAYING – CARING – SHARING

ALVIN J. VANDER GRIEND

Copyright © 2018 by Alvin J. Vander Griend

Scripture quotations in the main text not otherwise designated are from the HOLY BIBLE, NEW INTERNATIONAL VERSION ®, NIV®. Copyright © 1973, 1978, 1984, 2011 by International Bible Society. Scripture quotations in Appendix D: Seek and Find, are from the NEW INTERNATIONAL READERS VERSION, Copyright © 1995, 1996, 1998 by Biblica, Inc. Used by permission of Zondervan. All rights reserved worldwide.

Contents of this book may be reprinted with permission from Alvin J. Vander Griend, 606 Woodcreek Dr, Lynden, WA 98264

E-mail: Alvin@harvestprayer.com   Phone: 360-354-5072

Worldwide Publishing Group
7710-T Cherry Park Dr, Ste 224
Houston, TX 77095

http://WorldwidePublishingGroup.com
713-766-4271

ISBN: 978-0-9997837-0-2

Contents

Preface .... *ix*
Core Values .... *xi*
HOW TO USE THIS COURSE .... *xiii*
GROUP COMMITMENTS .... *xvii*

PART ONE: *Together* (Sessions 1-9)

1. The Power of Team 3
2. Love Never Fails 7
3. Building Each Other Up 11
4. Praying for Each Other 15
5. You Can Win over Sin 19
6. Shaped by the Word 23
7. Engaging the Enemy 27
8. Relying on the Spirit 31
9. Co-Working with Christ 35

PART TWO: Prayer (Sessions 10-14)

10. Great Things by Prayer 41
11. Pray for the Unsaved 45
12. Pray for Open Doors 49
13. Pray the Lord of Harvest 53
14. Setting Captives Free 57

PART THREE: Care (Sessions 15-20)

15. A Lifestyle of Love 63
16. Called to Serve 67
17. Make Friends for Christ 71
18. Let Your Light Shine 75
19. Be Wise Toward Outsiders 79
20. Be Quick to Listen 83

PART FOUR: Share (Sessions 21-29)

21. Lost People Matter to God 89
22. Your Life, His Story 93
23. What a Friend Is Jesus! 97
24. The Best News Ever 101
25. Turning Life Around 105
26. The Key Is Believing 109
27. The Word Does the Work 113
28. Steps to Receive Christ 117
29. Eternal Life Is a Gift 121

PART FIVE: Aftercare (Sessions 30-37)

30. Discipling New Christians 127
31. Vitally Linked to Christ 131
32. Experiencing God Through Prayer 135

33.	Living by the Word	139
34.	Devoted to One Another	143
35.	Finding a Place to Grow	147
36.	Sharing Life Together	151
37.	Qualified to Multiply	155

APPENDICES

A - My Loving People to Jesus List *159*
B - Ways to Pray for Seekers *161*
C - Prepare Your Personal Testimony *162*
D - Seek and Find *164*
E - Next Steps *181*

Preface

I created this devotional study--***Loving People to Jesus*** *by Praying, Caring, Sharing*—to help believers understand how God wins people to himself. It's about God's ability to work through ordinary people like you and me to reach our circles of influence—family members, friends, coworkers, and neighbors. It's about *prayer* that releases God's power and grace into their lives. It's about *caring* that channels God's love into aching, lonely hearts. It's about *sharing* the good news of salvation by grace with those who don't know him. It's about *teaming up* with others to win victories that no one of us could win on his or her own.

Why is *prayer* important in this process? Because prayer is the means by which divine power is released into people's lives. When the Bible says "prayer . . . is powerful and effective," it means God acts powerfully and effectively through the prayers of his people. When we pray for those in our circles of influence, we release God's life-changing power into their lives.

Why is *caring* important? We care because God cares. Caring communicates love. And the love we communicate by caring is a small sample of a greater love—God's love. We are channels of God's love to those for whom we care. No one comes to God unless they are in some way drawn by his love. People who experience God's love through us will be increasingly drawn to him.

Why is *sharing* important? The good news we share is the news of God's saving grace. It's the greatest news ever heard, the greatest gift ever offered—the gift of eternal life. It's news that brings to light the grace, the love, the joy, and the peace of God. It's news that has the power to transform the lives of friends who do not know Christ.

And why a team that works *together*? Loving our friends to Christ is something that we can do better together than alone. People working together can achieve results that individuals can't. It's one thing to practice shooting baskets in a gym; it's another to be part of a team that works together for a win. This is as true in evangelism as it is in basketball.

The people who work together in this course are a small group of believers who think, and plan, and pray, and work together to win people to Jesus. They pray for, care for, and share the good news with those in their circles of influence who don't know Christ. They follow through with *aftercare* for the newly committed, helping them become "fully mature in Christ" (Col. 1:28).

My hope and prayer is that you will together be used by the Lord to love many people to Jesus as you pray for them, care for them, and share the good news of Christ with them. *Alvin J. Vander Griend*

Core Values

WORD OF GOD: God reveals his will to us primarily through his Word. Small-group inductive Bible study is a way of digging deeply into the Word to discern God's heart and mind and to apply freshly gleaned truth to our personal lives. The small-group environment is important because we learn more and remember better if we wrestle with Scripture truths together. The Word of God will direct you as you love people to Jesus.

COVENANT COMMITMENT: Your praying, caring, sharing group is essentially a group of believers who covenant to support and strengthen each other spiritually in ways that will enhance your efforts to reach those who do not know Christ.

INTERCESSORY PRAYER: Your prayer-care-share team will double as an intercessory group. You will pray for each other to grow strong in the Lord; you will pray for caring hearts and caring opportunities; and you will pray for others in your circles of influence, especially those who appear to be spiritually disconnected.

LOVING CARE: The love of God, made available to us through Christ and the Holy Spirit, is the most powerful force in the world. God's love will saturate your lives and your ministries. God's love will flow to and through team members as you pray for each other and for those in your circles of influence. God's love will flow into the hearts and lives of non-believers who hear and embrace the good news.

GOSPEL SHARING: The good news of salvation through Jesus Christ is the best news the world has ever received. Good news shared and embraced has life-changing power. It is the means that God has given us to rescue the perishing, grow the church, and establish his kingdom here on earth. Sharing the gospel is the tip of the arrow for your praying, caring, sharing group.

DISCIPLING & ENFOLDING: Jesus commanded his followers to disciple others and to bring them to full obedience to his commands (Matt. 28:20). Scripture further challenges believers to "spur on one another to love and good deeds" and to encourage each other by meeting together regularly (Heb. 10:25). The *aftercare sessions* will help you disciple new believers and enfold them into the community of Christ.

HOW TO USE THIS COURSE

Forming a "Loving People to Jesus" Group.

- The ideal **size** for a "loving people to Jesus" group is three to five persons. If you have at least three, you will have the value of meaningful support fellowship. More than five will crowd the weekly 90-minute meeting agenda. Larger groups can be managed by breaking into smaller groups for parts of each session. For example, you could reflect on the opening devotional comments, read the **DISCOVER YOUR BIBLE** Scriptures and answer the **REFLECTION** with a group of twelve, then divide into three groups of four for the **GROUP SHARE TIME** and **GROUP PRAYER TIME**.
- If you are **forming a new group**, do so carefully and prayerfully. Begin by asking the Lord for one other person who is willing to join you. Then pray together and ask the Lord to lead you to additional members.

Group Covenant and Common Disciplines

The leader for the day reads the **Group Covenant** aloud at the beginning of each session (see Group Covenant and Common Disciplines on page?), and follows that with an opening prayer.

- The **Common Disciplines** should be shared at the first few sessions and periodically after that. Group members can share in the reading of these disciplines.

Timing

- "Loving people to Jesus" groups ordinarily meet weekly.
- The overall time spent in each session may vary from 60 to 90 minutes. Be alert to the suggested time frames for each segment. It's easy to miss important elements if these are not carefully guarded. Adhering to the suggested time will give you the greatest benefits. The facilitator should pace the group through each segment.
- The leader may choose to give time signals to the group or have another group member act as timekeeper.

Leader's Role

Group members may rotate as leaders. The leader should:
- Read the **Group Covenant** at the beginning of each session and lead the group in reading aloud the **Common Disciplines** at least once a month.
- Open the meeting with prayer.
- Walk the group through each segment of the session, pacing progress so that all key elements are given enough time. Try to involve everyone in the conversation, even if it means occasionally inviting specific members to comment.
- Help the group decide who will facilitate the next session.

During Group Sessions

- After the group covenant and opening prayer, group members share insights gathered from the session's opening devotional paragraphs. (5-10 minutes)
- Members participate in reading the **DISCOVER YOUR BIBLE** verses and share thoughts and insights stimulated by the **REFLECTION** questions. (15-25 minutes)
- Group members contribute personally in the **GROUP SHARE TIME**. (20-30 minutes)
- Members spend time in **GROUP PRAYER**, either praying for each other around the circle or covering all important joys and concerns in "popcorn prayer." (10-15 minutes)

Between Group Sessions

- Release God's power and blessing into each other's lives by praying *daily* for the members of your group.
- **LIVE OUT** the spiritual truths learned in each session by "praying the Word" and "living out the Word" in the intervening week(s).
- **LOOK AHEAD** to the next session and prepare by reading the opening devotional paragraphs. Mark words, sentences, or thoughts that strike you as particularly important or interesting. Be prepared to share your thoughts when the group convenes.
- Read and study the **DISCOVER YOUR BIBLE** passages for the next session. Note thoughts or questions that arise from verses. Use the **REFLECTION** questions to probe more deeply into the primary message of the Bible verses. Be prepared to share *your* reflections in your group session.
- Give special attention to what you will share in the **GROUP SHARE TIME** at the next session.

Multiply
During the last several weeks, invest prayer and discussion time into the possibility of starting one or more new "loving people to Jesus" groups. Ask the who, how, when, and why questions that need to be addressed (see session 37 for more specifics).

GROUP COMMITMENTS

Our Group Covenant

[The leader of the day opens each meeting with these words.]

Welcome to the *Loving People to Jesus* group. Remember that we meet together to grow stronger in the Lord and more effective in *praying* for, *caring* for, and *sharing* the good news of Christ with each other and with those in our spheres of influence. We do this by loving and supporting each other, by sharing ourselves as fully and openly as possible, and by holding each other accountable to life-giving spiritual disciplines. Everything we do and say in our meetings is to be held in confidence.

Common Disciplines

[Team members take turns reading the *Common Disciplines* aloud each month.]

- By God's grace, we will practice the presence of God by devoting ourselves to prayer and regular meditation on the Word of God.
- By God's grace, we will turn away from sin and will turn to God, and will find the refreshment that comes from him alone.
- By God's grace, we will seek to be filled with the knowledge of God's will through the wisdom and understanding of the Holy Spirit, so that we may live lives worthy of him and please him in every way.
- By God's grace, we will love each other as we are loved by Christ, and will increase and overflow in love for each other and for everyone else.
- By God's grace, we will befriend those in our circles of influence for Christ's sake, and will seek opportunities to share our faith with them and lead them to Christ.
- By God's grace, we will abide in Christ and hide his words in our hearts, so that we may bear much fruit to the Father's glory, showing ourselves to be his disciples.

PART ONE: Together (Sessions 1-9)

The first nine sessions of this devotional study will help you bond together in ways that will make you effective in loving people to Jesus. I encourage you to meet regularly as you work through these sessions and to share your lives as freely and honestly as possible. Embrace the Group Covenant and hold each other accountable to the life-giving Common Disciplines. In doing so, you will grow stronger in the Lord and more effective in the ministries of praying, caring, and sharing the good news. The encouragement and prayer support you receive from this group will make it possible for you to do together what you could never do alone.

Dig into God's Word together with the assurance that you will be trained in righteousness and "thoroughly equipped for every good work" (2 Tim. 3:16-17). Release God's power and grace into each other's lives through prayer. Study the Word and gain the wisdom, encouragement, and comfort that it promises. Gain vital victories over sin. Absorb afresh the assurance that love never fails. Build each other up in the most holy faith.

Your group will become a supportive fellowship. Together you'll discover what Solomon meant when he said, "As iron sharpens iron, so one person sharpens another" (Prov. 27:17). You'll find that "two are better than one. . . a cord of three strands is not quickly broken" (Eccl. 4:9, 12). You will live out the biblical challenge of Hebrews 10:24-25: "Let us consider how we may spur on one another toward love and good deeds, not giving up meeting together. . . but encouraging one another."

I pray that God will bless you in this venture and equip you, guide you, and empower you for life and for ministry.

SESSION 1

The Power of Team

Your "loving people to Jesus" group is coming together for two important reasons. *First,* to grow stronger in the Lord. *Second*, to be more effective in ministries of love to your friends and neighbors who need to know Christ. There are lots of things you can do very well alone. But when it comes to spiritual growth and effective ministry, you will do far better--up to ten times better--if you do it with other believers. That's the idea that undergirds this study.

There are many kinds of small groups in the church: prayer groups, Bible study groups, share groups, support groups, fellowship groups, and covenant groups. There is value in each of these. Your group will include all these elements. You will pray for each other at meetings and between meetings. You will discover fresh ideas from the Bible at every meeting and live out what you are learning between the meetings. You will enjoy deepening levels of friendship as you share your personal life journeys. You will covenant to support each other and hold each other accountable to agreed-upon disciplines. All these things you will do better together than you could possibly do alone.

Scripture emphasizes the value of working together. Moses teamed up with Joshua to lead Israel to the Promised Land. Aaron and Hur stood beside Moses to hold up his hands during battle. Daniel found support in three good friends—Hananiah, Mishael, and Azariah—and together they made a huge difference in the power center of the world. Solomon pointed out that "two are better than one . . . if either of them falls down, one can help the other up" (Eccl. 4:9-10). Jesus sent his disciples out in teams of two to practice ministry skills, and he took a support group of three with him to Gethsemane. The apostle Paul carried the gospel throughout the Gentile world with the help of many cohorts. Working together works better.

Years ago, I learned the value of this support in a personal way. The Lord led me into a support fellowship group with four other men. We met weekly to support and encourage each other in the Lord. We openly shared our lives with each other, studied God's Word together, prayed with and for each other, and held each other accountable to agreed-upon life goals. We covered each other in daily prayer that targeted our work, our relationships, our spiritual lives, our church and kingdom ministries, and all kinds of special needs. It turned out to be an awesome, life-changing experience for all of us. We soon found ourselves forging ahead spiritually and being catapulted into new and unexpected ministry opportunities.

The pilot group that first tested this devotional study had a similar experience. We kept our covenant with each other and found ourselves growing stronger in the Lord, gaining spiritual victories, and becoming more effective in ministry. We prayed for, cared for, and shared Christ with friends and acquaintances in ways that we could not have imagined before. My hope and prayer is that you will have a similar experience and that pre-Christians among your family members, friends, co-workers, and acquaintances will be touched by your prayers, will feel your love, and will come to know the love of your Savior and theirs.

In the **Together** sessions of the first nine weeks, you will share your lives as freely and honestly as possible and will gain spiritual strength and prayer support from each other. In the **Prayer** sessions that follow, you will create a prayer-care-share list of people who don't know Christ and will mount up strong prayer efforts on their behalf. In the **Care** sessions, you will major in building caring relationships with the people on your list and will prayerfully support each other in this effort. In the **Share** sessions, you will focus on ways to share the good news of Christ with a widening circle of folks, asking God to open doors of opportunity. Finally, in the **Aftercare** sessions, you will do everything you can to disciple and enfold those new to the faith.

Congratulations for taking on this challenge! I pray that you will be wonderfully blessed and greatly encouraged as you move forward in this prayer-based, love-motivated, gospel-inspired venture.

DISCOVER YOUR BIBLE

Proverbs 27:17
As iron sharpens iron, so one person sharpens another.

Ecclesiastes 4:9-12
Two are better than one because they have a good return for their labor: If either of them falls down, one can help the other up. But pity anyone who falls and has no one to help them up. Also, if two lie down together, they will keep warm. But how can one keep warm alone? Though one may be overpowered, two can defend themselves. A cord of three strands is not quickly broken.

Matthew 26:36-40
Then Jesus went with his disciples to a place called Gethsemane, and he said to them, "Sit here while I go over there and pray." He took Peter and the two sons of Zebedee along with him, and he began to be sorrowful and troubled. Then he said to them, "My soul is overwhelmed with sorrow to the point of death. Stay here and keep watch with me."
Going a little farther, he fell with his face to the ground and prayed, "My Father, if it is possible, may this cup be taken from me. Yet not as I will, but as you will."
Then he returned to his disciples and found them sleeping. "Couldn't you men keep watch with me for one hour?" he asked Peter.

Hebrews 10:24-25
And let us consider how we may spur one another on toward love and good deeds, not giving up meeting together, as some are in the habit of doing, but encouraging one another—and all the more as you see the Day approaching.

REFLECTION (15-20 minutes)

1. How do you expect to benefit from being part of a support group? What might be missing if you don't have the support of others?

2. What's the advantage of studying the Bible with others? Supporting each other in prayer? Engaging in ministry together?

3. Describe a time when you received the kind of help suggested in the above verses. Were there times you wanted support and didn't get it? Why was it missing?

4. What has to happen in a group in order for us to be spurred on to love and good deeds? What could cause a group to fail?

5. What is the value of accountability? Why might it sometimes be scary?

GROUP SHARE TIME (20-30 minutes)
Each person shares his or her personal history. Include where you were born, your birth family, schooling, marriage, current family, and jobs you have held. [5-6 minutes each.] Each person also shares personal joys and concerns to be covered in the group prayer time.

GROUP PRAYER TIME (10-15 minutes)
Group members give thanks to God for the life blessings shared by each person and also remember before God the joys and concerns of each person.

LIVE IT OUT (between meetings)
- Regularly remember your group members in prayer. Give thanks for God's leading in their lives.
- Pray the Scriptures studied in Session 1, turning God's words into prayers of praise, thanks, confession, petition, and intercession.
- Live out the Word by *sharpening each other, helping each other, praying for each other,* and *spurring each other on.*

LOOK AHEAD (before the next meeting)
- Thoughtfully read the opening comments of Session 2.
- Discover the Bible's thoughts on *love never fails.*
- Think through the contribution you will make in the GROUP SHARE TIME at the next session.

PERSONAL NOTES

SESSION 2
Love Never Fails

You are part of a fellowship group that is bonded together in love. The love you experience in your group will be more than a feeling. It is our concern for each other expressed in commitment and action. The Apostle John thought of love in terms of action: "Dear children, let us not love with words or speech but with actions and in truth." To love this way is to choose the highest good of the person loved.

Imagine for a moment that your group is devoted to loving you with that kind of love. They *value you* above themselves and *look to your interests* above their own (Phil. 2:3-4). They even *honor you* above themselves (Rom. 12:10). They love you so deeply that they are even willing to *overlook the sin-flaws* in your life (1 Pet. 4:8). And, the truth is, you are being called to love each one of your group friends in the same way. You are committed to doing everything possible to make sure that they are abundantly blessed. What an amazing experience it is to be part of such a group!

But that is exactly what Christ intended life to be like for his followers. He both commanded and modeled this love: "A new command I give you: love one another. As I have loved you, you must also love one another" (John 13:34). His Word established it as the highest of all virtues: "Now these three remain: faith, hope and love. But the greatest of these is love" (1 Cor. 13:13). Paul prayed that Christ-followers would be "rooted and grounded in love" (Eph. 3:16) and would wear love like an over-garment that binds other virtues together in perfect unity (Col. 3:14).

Such love was, in fact, to be *the* distinguishing mark of his disciples. He said: "By this everyone will know that you are my disciples, if you love one another" (John 13:35). Philosophers were known in Jesus' day by their distinctive theories of life. Epicureans were known for pleasure-seeking. Stoics were known for their ability to endure pain or hardship without showing their feelings. Christ's disciples, however, were to be known for their love for one another.

But this kind of love is not simply for our inner circle of friends. It is this very love that drives us beyond our usual boundaries of relationships to those outside the margins of Christ's love. Love causes us to be other-minded and to focus attention on those who need it most. We become love distributors who willingly give our time, talents and treasures to those in need of true love. The love-impoverished world that has not yet known the love of Christ is far more impressed by such love than by our lofty creeds, our stately buildings or our sacred worship services.

Few things will help us reach out with love and care more than experiencing the love of Christ within a small circle of loving friends. So as you meet each week, relish the love-support you receive from each other, and remember the wider world that desperately needs what you have. Be prepared to give it away.

DISCOVER YOUR BIBLE

John 13:34-35
"A new command I [Jesus] give you: Love one another. As I have loved you, so you must love one another. By this everyone will know that you are my disciples, if you love one another."

Romans 12:9-10
Love must be sincere. Hate what is evil; cling to what is good. Be devoted to one another in love. Honor one another above yourselves.

1 Corinthians 13:4-8
Love is patient, love is kind. It does not envy, it does not boast, it is not proud. It does not dishonor others, it is not self-seeking, it is not easily angered, it keeps no record of wrongs. Love does not delight in evil but rejoices with the truth. It always protects, always trusts, always hopes, always perseveres. Love never fails. But where there are prophecies, they will cease; where there are tongues, they will be stilled; where there is knowledge, it will pass away.

Philippians 2:1-4
Therefore if you have any encouragement from being united with Christ, if any comfort from his love, if any common sharing in the Spirit, if any tenderness and compassion, then make my joy complete by being like-minded, having the same love, being one in spirit and of one mind. Do nothing out of selfish ambition or vain conceit. Rather, in humility value others above yourselves, not looking to your own interests but each of you to the interests of the others.

1 John 3:18
Dear children, let us not love with words or speech but with actions and in truth.

REFLECTION (15-20 minutes)

1. Read John 13:34-35 slowly and thoughtfully substituting the words "choose the highest good for" in place of the word love. How does reading it that way affect your understanding of love?

2. Is it really possible for us to love as Jesus loved? Why or why not? What will it cost us to love as Jesus loved? What will be gained?

3. Why will others know that we are Jesus disciples if we love each other? Do we give them the right to think otherwise if we don't love each other?

4. What is the practical value of being in a support group where members are committed to always protect you, always trust you, always value you, and always look to your interests no matter what?

5. What can make it hard to choose the highest good for another person? How can you overcome that difficulty?

GROUP SHARE TIME (20-30 minutes)
Whose unfailing love has done more than most to shape your life for good (think of parents, teachers, pastors, friends, coworkers, etc.)? Briefly tell how one or two people made a big difference in your life.

Each person also shares personal reasons for thanks and prayer requests.

GROUP PRAYER TIME (10-15 minutes)
Praise God for his love, remembering especially how that love has reached you through others. Cover the requests of each person and give thanks with them for God's blessings.

LIVE IT OUT (between meetings)
- Continue to cover group members in prayer. Thank God for each person whose influence has shaped your life for good.
- Pray the Word by turning God's words from Session 2 into prayers of praise, thanks, confession, petition and intercession.
- Live out the Word by *loving one another, honoring one another,* and *looking to the interests of one another.*

LOOK AHEAD (before the next meeting)
- Thoughtfully read the opening comments of Session 3,
- Discover the Bible's thoughts on *building each other up,*
- Think through the contribution you will make in the GROUP SHARE TIME at the next session.

PERSONAL NOTES

SESSION 3

Building Each Other Up

As Christians, we are up against far more than we can handle alone. But, praise the Lord, we don't have to "do life" alone. We "can do everything through [Christ] who gives [us] strength" (Phil. 4:13). One important way Christ's strength becomes ours is through friends who come alongside.

Soldiers don't go into war alone. They go surrounded by battle buddies who fight beside them and for them. In the face of trials and temptations, we need battle buddies to pray with us, to share our burdens and to hold us accountable to godly standards. With their help, we can guard our hearts, deal with weaknesses and failures, achieve integrity, and guard against unhealthy relationships. Spiritual partners have enormous positive consequences for our lives.

Scripture often refers to such relationships. David and Jonathan formed a bond that strengthened them both. Solomon wrote that "a friend...sticks closer than a brother" (Prov. 18:24) and that "as iron sharpens iron, so one man sharpens another" (Prov. 27:17). Paul encourages us to "carry each other's burdens" (Gal. 6:2) and to "make every effort to build each other up" (Rom. 14:19). Being accountable to one another is a good way to make these kinds of relationships work.

To make your fellowship group work you need to meet regularly and build personal relationships. Pursue together the development of basic Christian virtues and disciplines like prayer, meditation on Scripture, faith sharing, nurturing the fruit of the Spirit, and doing acts of service. Be sensitive to and supportive of the others. Trust yourselves to each other, by degrees, as freely and honestly as possible. Share your personal and spiritual journeys, your relationships at home and work, your strengths and weaknesses, and your goals in life. Don't be afraid to reveal what is really going on in your hearts and lives. Keep the limits of confidentiality decided upon by the group. And remember to give these relationships time. Meaningful spiritual support doesn't happen overnight.

Fellowship groups meet real and personal needs in important ways. Members discover--many for the first time--the true meaning of "communion of the saints." They find the love that every heart cries out for. They discover that the love that flows from other believers is really the love of Christ channeled to them through another person.

One member of a newly formed fellowship group testified: "The sharing is what made the group special. It allowed love to flow. I found the more I could share, the more I understood myself. On the other side, when I was able to listen and support a brother, I received as much as he did. I felt worth and joy within myself that I could reach out and touch someone else. I can feel the love of Christ."

DISCOVER YOUR BIBLE

1 Samuel 20:41-42
After the boy had gone, David got up from the south side of the stone and bowed down before Jonathan three times, with his face to the ground. Then they kissed each other and wept together—but David wept the most.
Jonathan said to David, "Go in peace, for we have sworn friendship with each other in the name of the LORD, saying, 'The LORD is witness between you and me, and between your descendants and my descendants forever.'" Then David left, and Jonathan went back to the town.
[For the complete story of David & Jonathan read 1 Samuel 20.}

Proverbs 17:17
A friend loves at all times, and a brother is born for a time of adversity.

Proverbs 18:24
One who has unreliable friends soon comes to ruin, but there is a friend who sticks closer than a brother.

Romans 14:19
So let us do all we can to live in peace. And let us work hard to build up one another (NIRV).

Galatians 6:2
Carry each other's burdens, and in this way you will fulfill the law of Christ.

REFLECTION (15-20 minutes)

1. What, according to the above verses, do true friends do for each other? Why do you think the Bible emphasizes the importance of friendship?

2. What is there about "sworn" friendship that can easily be translated into the values of a covenant group?

3. Why might a person with unreliable friends come to ruin (Prov. 18:24)? What might keep people from having truly helpful friends?

4. In what areas of your life do you most want or need to be built up?

5. What appeals to you most about being part of a support group?

GROUP SHARE TIME (20-30 minutes)
Tell your group about a good friend whose influence has done more than most others to build you up. What did they do that helped the most? What gains did you make as a result of their help?

Share the personal prayer requests and spiritual goals for which you would like prayer support.

GROUP PRAYER TIME (10-15 minutes)
Continue to pray for the known requests of each person and give thanks with them for those through whom they were built up. Pray for the spiritual goals that each person identified in the group share time.

LIVE IT OUT (between meetings)
- Give thanks to God for each person in your group, and for the blessing you are to each other as God binds your hearts and lives together. Continue to build up fellow group members through prayer.
- Pray the Word_by integrating ideas from the Bible passages studied into your ongoing prayers.
- Live out the Scriptures you have studied by *sticking close to your friends, building each other up,* and *carrying each other's burdens.*

LOOK AHEAD (before the next meeting)
- Thoughtfully read the opening comments of Session 4.
- Discover the Bible's thoughts on *praying for each other*.
- Think through the contribution you will make in the GROUP SHARE TIME at the next session.

PERSONAL NOTES

SESSION 4
Praying for Each Other

As a support group, you are committed to love one another and to build each other up. One of the primary ways that you can do that is through praying for each other. Your supportive prayers will go far beyond the ordinary prayer support you would expect from the broader Christian community. They will touch the deep-level realities of your life: your emotional scars, relational challenges, spiritual struggles and real-life temptations—the kinds of things you share with your group that you wouldn't share publicly.

As you come to know each other well and care for each other deeply, your feelings for each other will be reflected in your prayers. Deep love tends to elicit constant, heartfelt prayers. Paul, who said to the Philippian believers, "I have you in my heart" and "I long for you all with the affection of Christ" (Phil, 1:7-8), prayed for them constantly with joy, and with confidence that God was at work in their lives (Phil. 1:6, 9-11).

Focused prayer can make a *huge difference*. Consider the life-changing difference that Epaphras's prayer made for the Colossian Christians: "that they might stand firm in all the will of God, mature and fully assured" (Col. 4:12). Imagine what happened in the lives of Thessalonian believers as Paul prayed that they might be worthy of God's calling and asked God to "bring to fruition . . . every desire for goodness and every deed prompted by faith" (2 Thess. 1:12).

I have a couple of raised garden plots in my back yard. The strawberries, beans, peas, and tomatoes that grow in those beds get special attention. They get composted soil, special fertilizers, careful weeding and plenty of water. They get a lot more attention than the rest of the back yard. And they show it. Things really grow in those beds. It's like that when you walk together in life with a small group of Christians and pray vigorously for each other. You get special attention and you grow strong together.

The prayers of a support group also provide *protection* from the evil one. Satan, bent on our destruction, goes about "like a roaring lion looking for someone to devour" (1 Pet. 5:8). God, intent on our salvation, supplies protection in response to prayer. When Simon Peter was being tested by Satan, Jesus came to his defense: "I have prayed for you, Simon, that your faith may not fail" (Lk. 22:32). By means of prayer we can thwart the devil's designs in the lives of our fellow group members. It's no wonder that the devil fears our prayers more than anything else. An unknown author and mighty prayer warrior once said, "There is nothing the devil dreads so much as prayer . . . 'Satan laughs at our toiling, mocks at our wisdom, but trembles when we pray'"

Jesus placed great value on believers praying together. He said, "If two of you on earth agree about anything you ask for, it will be done for you by my Father in heaven" (Matt. 18:19). In other words, when believers agree together in prayer, things will happen on earth that otherwise would not have happened.

God chooses to work in response to prayer. His Word challenges us to "lift up holy hands" (1 Tim. 2:8) on behalf of others. When you do so, your support group will have spiritual strength you never dreamed possible.

DISCOVER YOUR BIBLE

Matthew 18:19-20
"Again, truly I tell you that if two of you on earth agree about anything they ask for, it will be done for them by my Father in heaven. For where two or three gather in my name, there am I with them."

Romans 15:30
I urge you, brothers and sisters, by our Lord Jesus Christ and by the love of the Spirit, to join me in my struggle by praying to God for me.

Colossians 4:12
Epaphras, who is one of you and a servant of Christ Jesus, sends greetings. He is always wrestling in prayer for you, that you may stand firm in all the will of God, mature and fully assured.

2 Thessalonians 1:11-12
With this in mind, we constantly pray for you, that our God may make you worthy of his calling, and that by his power he may bring to fruition your every desire for goodness and your every deed prompted by faith. We pray this so that the name of our Lord Jesus may be glorified in you, and you in him.

James 5:16
Pray for each other.... The prayer of a righteous person is powerful and effective.

REFLECTION (15-20 minutes)

1. How can two or more believers arrive at agreement in prayer? Why might agreement in prayer make a difference in the way God responds (Matt.18:19-20)?

2. What does it mean to wrestle in prayer? If you do wrestle in prayer, who are you wrestling with? Tell your group about a time when you wrestled in prayer.

3. Are the intercessory prayers mentioned in the above verses mostly reactive or proactive? What outcomes are expected from the proactive prayers?

4. What kinds of proactive prayers might your group continually pray for each other?

5. Would you like to have a Paul or Epaphras praying for you? Why? Is that possible today?

GROUP SHARE TIME (20-30 minutes)
Share with your group two or three personal spiritual goals for which you would like them to pray.

Each person shares joys and concerns in preparation for the group prayer time.

GROUP PRAYER TIME (10-15 minutes)
Cover the ongoing joys and concerns of your covenant group, and pray for the spiritual goals of each person.

LIVE IT OUT (between meetings)
- Continue to pray daily for each person in your group, remembering especially their spiritual goals.
- Pray the Word by lifting up prayer thoughts to God that arise from the Scriptures you studied in this session.
- Live out the Word by *wrestling in prayer for each other so that each of you may be well grounded, spiritually mature, strong in faith,* and *fruitful.*

LOOK AHEAD (before the next meeting)
- Thoughtfully read the opening comments of Session 5.
- Discover the Bible's thoughts on how *you can win over sin.*
- Think through the contribution you will make in the GROUP SHARE TIME at the next session.

PERSONAL NOTES

SESSION 5
You Can Win over Sin

Everybody wants to win. Children want to win their games. Baseball players want to win the World Series. Football teams are known to give everything to win the Super Bowl. And sports fans count their teams' wins as their own.

God wants to win too, and he *has* won. He has won the greatest victory of all—the win over sin. He has won it for us, his children, through the death of his Son on the cross. He invites us to step into that win with him, to claim it as our own. And though he has won, and we have won with him, the game is not over. We continue to do battle with sin every day, and by his grace we are able to win the ongoing battle with sin.

The Son of God is our coach, a coach who both directs us and empowers us by his Spirit to win over sin. And prayer is the action by which his guidance is secured and his power released over the world, the flesh and the devil. That win is bigger than the World Series or the Super Bowl. Really! It's the win of a lifetime, an eternal lifetime. You can do it! You can win over sin. So go for it!

Sin, according to the Bible, is missing the mark of God's standard for our lives. That sounds like simply breaking a law; but it's worse than that. It's breaking a relationship with the most important Person in our lives: God. It's rebelling against God, distrusting his promises and spurning his love. Some sins are flagrant actions, like sexual immorality, murder, theft or drunkenness. However, more common—especially among believers—are subtle sins like pride, lust, envy, slander, deceit and selfish ambition. Whether flagrant or subtle, all sin is equally displeasing to God.

Sin has tragic consequences, especially when it comes to our relationship with God. It separates us from God, hinders prayer, and robs us of the pleasure of his presence. Sin deprives us of God-intended blessings and sows the seeds of anxiety, fear, loneliness, failure and despair. If not dealt with, sin has the power to cause suffering, spiritual blindness, hardness of heart, guilt, and shame; it leads inevitably to God's judgment. Sin is our biggest problem. Sin has been the undoing of the human race. All sin must be dealt with if we are to avoid ruin and destruction.

But there is hope—hope for overcoming both the guilt and the impurity of sin. Overcoming starts with confession: "If we confess our sins, he [God] is faithful and just and will forgive our sins and purify us from all unrighteousness" (1 John 1:9). Overcoming continues with repentance—turning away from sin and returning to our love relationship with God.

There is also hope for overcoming the *power* of sin—that lethal force that operates through the world, the flesh, and the devil. Having been crucified with Christ, we have victory over our sinful natures and are "no longer slaves to sin" (Rom. 6:6). Through our faith in Christ we have victory over the world (1 John 5:4-5). And because the Son of God appeared to destroy the devil's work, we are delivered from him too (Matt. 6:13).

Judith Viorst titled her notable children's book *Alexander and the Terrible, Horrible, No Good, Very Bad Day*. Let me say, echoing her title, that sin is a terrible, horrible, no good, very bad thing. It is terrible because it can lead to daily devastation. Worse than that, if not forgiven and canceled, it leads to eternal destruction.

Study the following verses with an awareness that God hates sin and opposes every shape and form it may take. Learn how, with God's help, you can do battle with sin whenever and wherever it may touch your life. You *can* overcome! You *can* win over sin! You *can* live a victorious Christian life!

DISCOVER YOUR BIBLE

Proverbs 28:13
Whoever conceals their sins does not prosper, but the one who confesses and renounces them finds mercy.

1 John 1:9
If we confess our sins, he is faithful and just and will forgive us our sins and purify us from all unrighteousness.

Romans 6:6-7, 11-12
For we know that our old self was crucified with him so that the body ruled by sin might be done away with, that we should no longer be slaves to sin—because anyone who has died has been set free from sin. . . . In the same way, count yourselves dead to sin but alive to God in Christ Jesus. Therefore, do not let sin reign in your mortal body so that you obey its evil desires.

1 John 2:15-17
Do not love the world or anything in the world. If anyone loves the world, love for the Father is not in them. For everything in the world—the lust of the flesh, the lust of the eyes, and the pride of life—comes not from the Father but from the world. The world and its desires pass away, but whoever does the will of God lives forever.

James 4:7
Submit yourselves, then, to God. Resist the devil, and he will flee from you.

REFLECTION (15-20 minutes)

1. According to these verses, how can we win over sin? Why is winning over sin so important?

2. What does it mean to be slaves to sin? How can we be set free? What does it mean to be free from sin?

3. How does being free from sin affect the way we think of ourselves? How might our freedom affect the decisions we make?

4. How would you define "world"? Why is it impossible to love both the Father and the world at the same time? How will your choice of what to love affect your life?

5. What are you going to do to defeat the devil? What can your group do to help you win over sin?

GROUP SHARE TIME (20-30 minutes)
What battles with sin are you fighting right now for which you need the prayer-help of your group? How would you like your covenant partners to pray?

Also, share personal prayer requests and expressions of gratitude.

GROUP PRAYER TIME (10-15 minutes)
Group members each share a personal prayer in which you *repent* of any known sins and claim God's forgiveness, in which you *thank* God for giving you *victory over sin*, and in which you ask for God's help to crucify the flesh, overcome the world and resist the devil.

Also, pray for each other asking that each of you may, "be strong in the Lord and in his might power" in the face of temptation (Eph. 6:10).

LIVE IT OUT (between meetings)
- Continue to lift each other up in prayer, remembering especially personal requests and areas of temptation.
- Pray the Word as revealed in the Bible passages studied in this session.
- Live out the Word by *confessing and renouncing any sin you are aware of, not letting sin reign in you, and submitting yourself to God.*

LOOK AHEAD (before the next meeting)
- Thoughtfully read the opening comments of Session 6.
- Discover the Bible's thoughts on *shaped by the Word.*
- Think about the contribution you will make in the GROUP SHARE TIME at the next session.

PERSONAL NOTES

SESSION 6
Shaped by the Word

We all know that the Word of God is absolutely essential for personal growth. It shapes our lives by providing wisdom, encouragement, inspiration and comfort. This happens as we read and meditate on the Word personally and regularly.

It also happens as we read and reflect with others. Light shines into our lives directly from the Word—but also through the thoughts and words of believing friends. Scripture teaches that the Word "is a lamp to [our] feet and a light for [our] path" (Ps. 119:105). But it also teaches us that believers are "the light of the world" and are meant to "shine before men" (Matt. 5:14, 16). Studying Scripture with other believers gives us two sources of light—the Word itself and the light that shines through other Christ-followers. Think of walking on a path in the dark of night with a flashlight. Great! You can see your way. But then add to that a few luminous persons who shine like angels. With them beside you, walking in the dark gets even better.

Several things happen as we study the Word of God together. First, the Word *exposes sin* in our lives. It "is living and active . . . penetrating even to dividing soul and spirit . . . it judges the thoughts and attitudes of the heart" (Heb. 4:12-13). The God-breathed Scriptures are useful, says Paul, "for . . . rebuking and correcting" (2 Tim. 3:16). The Word can penetrate to the center of our being and expose the hidden depths of our secret selves. In so doing it brings us again and again to the One who has solved the sin problem and can help us deal with the realities of life in this world.

Second, God's Word is profitable for *teaching*. It teaches us what is true about God, about our world, and about ourselves. It gives us accurate information about the unseen world of angels, demons, heaven, hell and life after death. It sheds light on love, money, sex, friendship, work, marriage, parenting and a host of other topics. It will keep us from making umpteen mistakes. It contains all that we need to know for life and happiness. What a treasure! Theodore Roosevelt said: "A thorough knowledge of the Bible is worth more than a college education".

Third, the Bible will equip us for *service*. Though we're born with a sinful nature that makes us prone to selfishness, pride, and addictions, God uses Scripture to bring us into a state of grace and to become his workmanship, "thoroughly equipped for every good work" (2 Tim. 3:17).

Fourth, the "Book," if allowed to shape our thoughts and our lives, will produce *prosperity and success*. These words from Joshua 1:8 are not a promise of financial wealth or worldly success. Instead they promise a life that abounds with personal, relational, and spiritual blessings. The Word has the power to transform, to produce fruit, and to give us abundant life.

For these things to happen, the Word must get into us. Studying the Bible with a group of friends will move us from thinking about the passage to stepping into the passage. It will allow the Holy Spirit to shape us from the inside out, so that our lives truly reflect the Living Word.

DISCOVER YOUR BIBLE

Joshua 1:8
"Keep this Book of the Law always on your lips; meditate on it day and night, so that you may be careful to do everything written in it. Then you will be prosperous and successful."

Psalm 1:1-3
Blessed is the one . . . whose delight is in the law of the LORD, and who meditates on his law day and night. That person is like a tree planted by streams of water, which yields its fruit in season and whose leaf does not wither—whatever they do prospers.

2 Timothy 3:16-17
All Scripture is God-breathed and is useful for teaching, rebuking, correcting and training in righteousness, so that the servant of God may be thoroughly equipped for every good work.

Hebrews 5:13-14
Anyone who lives on milk, being still an infant, is not acquainted with the teaching about righteousness. But solid food is for the mature, who by constant use have trained themselves to distinguish good from evil.

REFLECTION (15-20 minutes)

1. What benefits do we gain from the Word of God if we use it properly?

2. What do we have to do with the Word of God to reap the benefits promised? Why isn't it enough to simply read the Bible?

3. What is there about our world today that hinders serious Bible study? If a person who delights in the Word is "like a tree planted by streams of water," what does a person who neglects the Word look like?

4. What Bible study methods work best for you? What tends to hinder your use of the Word?

5. What are the benefits of studying the Bible with other believers in a support group? Can small-group Bible study help a person delight in and meditate on on the Word of God? If so, how?

GROUP SHARE TIME (20-30 minutes)
Share with your group two or three Bible passages God has used to shape your spiritual life. What changes took place?

Share personal prayer requests and reasons for thanksgiving.

GROUP PRAYER TIME (10-15 minutes)
Pray prayers of intercession and thanksgiving over each person in the group, covering the items that have been shared. Give thanks especially for the ways in which the Word of God has shaped each person's life, and ask God to continue to transform each of you through his Word.

LIVE IT OUT (between meetings)
- Regularly cover each other's joys and concerns in prayer.
- <u>Pray through the Bible passages</u> that you studied for this session, finding reasons for thanksgiving to God.
- <u>Live out the Word</u> by *spending time in it; delighting in it; being careful to do everything written in it;* and *being taught, rebuked, corrected, trained and equipped by the Scriptures.*

LOOK AHEAD (before the next meeting)
- Thoughtfully read the opening comments of Session 7.
- Discover the Bible's thoughts on *engaging the enemy.*
- Think through the contribution you will make in the GROUP SHARE TIME at the next session.

PERSONAL NOTES

SESSION 7
Engaging the Enemy

Almost every time you watch the evening news on TV there will be both good news and bad news. Time and again when you read the words of Scripture there will also be good news and bad. There is the *good news* of God's saving work through Jesus Christ, and the *bad news* of enemy atrocities carried out by the spiritual forces of evil in the heavenly realms. The Bible calls Satan "the god of this world" (2 Cor. 4:4), which means that he is still very powerful and that he claims--though falsely--the world as his territory.

This is bad news! We live in a world where evil is rampant. We have a terrible enemy—the devil. He is powerful, cunning, and supernatural. He has great numbers of demons ready to fight his battles. His ways are deceitful and destructive. He prowls around like a roaring lion (1 Peter 5:8) or masquerades as an "angel of light" (2 Cor.11:14). He is working night and day to destroy the church and diminish the glory of Christ. To put it bluntly, life for believers in the world today is war.

If we establish the kingdom of God and spread the good news, we will face strong opposition. Jesus gives us three powerful ways to deal with our fiendish enemy. First, we have *prayer*. James stresses the fact that our prayers are "powerful and effective" (James 5:16). Samuel Chadwick contended: "Satan dreads nothing but prayer. His one concern is to keep the saints from praying. He fears nothing from prayerless studies, prayerless work, prayerless religion. He laughs at our toil, he mocks our wisdom, but he trembles when we pray." Satan dreads our prayers because prayer moves the arm of God, and that is the one thing he cannot defeat.

Second, we can invade Satan's domain with a power that is greater than any power at his disposal—the *power of love*. On his way to the cross Jesus declared, "Now the prince of this world will be driven out. But I, when I am lifted up will draw all men to myself" (John 12:31-32). It was the power of love that conquered the prince of darkness and drew us to Christ. That same love compels us to build bridges that bring freedom and life-change to friends and neighbors.

The third power that we wield is *the power of the gospel*. Paul said it with clarity and simplicity in Romans 1:16: "The gospel. . .is the power of God for the salvation of everyone who believes." It is the good news of Christ, a message of salvation. It has life-changing power. It is for everyone. Today there are over one billion followers of Christ in the world who can testify to the life-changing power of that gospel. Satan's domain is crumbling.

The good news is that we are winning the battle. Jesus came not only to seek and save the lost but to "destroy the devil's work" (1 John 3:8). Paul reminds us that Christ "disarmed the powers and authorities . . . triumphing over them by the cross" (Col. 2:15). And the author of Hebrews stresses that Jesus "[destroyed] him who holds the power of death—that is, the devil—and [freed] those who all their lives were held in slavery by their fear of death" (Heb. 2:14-15). Praise the Lord!

So remember, as you engage the enemy, that you are on the winning side. Christ has won the victory. Our archenemy is defeated. You are now involved in the mop-up operation. Make use of your special weapons: "Finally, be strong in the Lord and in his mighty power. Put on the full armor of God so that you can take your stand against the devil's schemes" (Eph. 6:10-11).

DISCOVER YOUR BIBLE

Matthew 13:19
"When anyone hears the message about the kingdom and does not understand it, the evil one comes and snatches away what was sown in their heart."

Acts 10:38
"God anointed Jesus of Nazareth with the Holy Spirit and power, and how he went around doing good and healing all who were under the power of the devil, because God was with him."

2 Corinthians 4:4
The god of this age has blinded the minds of unbelievers, so that they cannot see the light of the gospel that displays the glory of Christ, who is the image of God.

2 Corinthians 10:3-5
For though we live in the world, we do not wage war as the world does. The weapons we fight with are not the weapons of the world. On the contrary, they have divine power to demolish strongholds. We demolish arguments and every pretension that sets itself up against the knowledge of God, and we take captive every thought to make it obedient to Christ.

Ephesians 6:10-12
Finally, be strong in the Lord and in his mighty power. Put on the full armor of God, so that you can take your stand against the devil's schemes. For our struggle is not against flesh and blood, but against the rulers, against the authorities, against the powers of this dark world and against the spiritual forces of evil in the heavenly realms.

1 John 3:8
The reason the Son of God appeared was to destroy the devil's work.

REFLECTION (15-20 minutes)

1. How is the devil trying to keep Christ from building his kingdom? Are his efforts working?

2. What has Christ done to defeat the enemy? How is he currently working to defeat the devil?

3. What is our role in defeating the enemy? What does it mean to "demolish strongholds"?

4. What are the weapons with which we fight? How do our weapons compare to the weapons of the world? What can we do to be more effective in thwarting the devil's efforts?

GROUP SHARE TIME (20-30 minutes)

What spiritual weapons have you found to be the most effective in dealing with the enemy? What spiritual victories have you won? Share these with your group.

Share personal prayer requests and any challenges you may be facing in the realm of spiritual warfare.

GROUP PRAYER TIME (10-15 minutes)

Cover each other in prayer and give thanks for victories won.

Pray that you may individually and corporately be strong in the Lord and the strength of his might.

LIVE IT OUT (between meetings)
- Pray faithfully for the members of your group, especially supporting them in the battles they've mentioned.
- Pray the Word and find strength in the Lord as you prayerfully engage in spiritual warfare.
- Live out the Word by *being strong in the Lord and in his mighty power, and by putting on the full armor of God.*

LOOK AHEAD (before the next meeting)
- Thoughtfully read the opening comments of Session 8.
- Discover the Bible's thoughts on *relying on the Spirit*.
- Think through the contribution you will make in the GROUP SHARE TIME at the next session.

PERSONAL NOTES

SESSION 8
Relying on the Spirit

Why did God send the Holy Spirit? There are many ways to answer that question. The most obvious is the one given by Jesus: "I will ask the Father, and he will give you another Counselor to be with you forever—the Spirit of truth . . . he lives with you and will be in you" (John 14:16-17). Jesus is assuring his followers—including us--that the Spirit will take his place as teacher and guide.

Beyond that, the Spirit equips us to spread the gospel. Even after three years' training under Jesus, there was no way the disciples could do the work of evangelism without the Holy Spirit. Aware of that impossibility, Jesus said, "I am going to send you what my Father has promised; but stay in the city until you have been clothed with power from on high" (Luke 24:49). In other words, Jesus was saying, "Without the Spirit don't even try!" As he left them, he said, "You will receive power when the Holy Spirit comes on you; and you will be my witnesses in Jerusalem, and in all Judea and Samaria, and to the ends of the earth" (Acts 1:8).

We cannot be effective witnesses for Christ without the all-powerful, all-wise, everywhere present, indwelling Holy Spirit. We too must be clothed with power from on high.

There are at least three ways in which the Spirit helps us witness effectively. First, he provides the *power*. As Jesus promised, the disciples received this power at Pentecost when "all of them were filled with the Holy Spirit." Peter used this newly released power to deliver a message to the gathered crowd that resulted in about three thousand being added to the church. Later God used Barnabas, a man "full of the Holy Spirit and faith," to bring a great number of people to the Lord in Antioch (Acts 11:24). Paul, God's chosen apostle to the Gentiles, gave credit to the power of the Holy Spirit for the spread of the gospel in Thessalonica (I Thess. 1:5).

Second, the Spirit provides the *message*. The Spirit of truth, said Jesus, "will guide you into all truth. He will not speak on his own; he will speak only what he hears, and he will tell you what is yet to come" (John 16:13). Paul reached his listeners "not in words taught by human wisdom but in words taught by the Spirit" (1 Cor. 2:11-13).

But there is one more thing that needs to happen if the message is to make an impact. It must be conveyed. It must get out of our Spirit-empowered hearts and our truth-enlightened head to those who will hear. I call this *outflow*. It's what Jesus was talking about when he said, "Whoever believes in me, as the Scripture has said, streams of living water will flow from within him." John explains, "By this he meant the Spirit, whom those who believed in him were later to receive" (John 7:38-39). In other words, it's the Holy Spirit who creates the outflow and blesses the hearer with a life-giving drink.

There is no way that we can achieve our faith-sharing goals based on what *we* can bring to the witnessing situation. We need, above all, the Holy Spirit's enabling power to achieve the otherwise impossible. God stands ready and willing to give us the help we need. We only need to ask. "How much more," said Jesus, comparing his heavenly Father to earthly parents, "will your Father in heaven given the Holy Spirit to those who ask him" (Luke 11:13). So, go ahead and ask. The Father is waiting.

DISCOVER YOUR BIBLE

Zechariah 4:6
This is the word of the LORD to Zerubbabel: "Not by might nor by power, but by my Spirit," says he Lord.

Luke 24:49
"I am going to send you what my Father has promised; but stay in the city until you have been clothed with power from on high."

John 7:38-39
Whoever believes in me, as Scripture has said, rivers of living water will flow from within them." By this he meant the Spirit, whom those who believed in him were later to receive.

John 16:13-14
"But when he, the Spirit of truth, comes, he will guide you into all the truth. He will not speak on his own; he will speak only what he hears, and he will tell you what is yet to come. He will glorify me because it is from me that he will receive what he will make known to you."

1 Corinthians 2:12-13
We have received . . . the Spirit who is from God, so that we may understand what God has freely given us. This is what we speak, not in words taught us by human wisdom but in words taught by the Spirit, explaining spiritual realities with Spirit-taught words.

REFLECTION (15-20 minutes)

1. Why do we need the help of the Holy Spirit to share our faith? What will be missing if the Spirit is not involved?

2. What are some things that the Holy Spirit does to help us communicate the gospel? Why can't we do this without his help?

3. What practically must we do to receive the help of the Holy Spirit?

4. How will those with whom we share benefit if we witness with Spirit-taught words?

5. If the Spirit flows from us like a "rivers of living water," what will the effect be on those in our circles of influence?

GROUP SHARE TIME (20-30 minutes)

What kind of help would you most like to receive from the Holy Spirit: fruit (Gal. 5:22-23), power (Lk. 24:49), guidance (Jn. 16:13-14), a message (Jn. 14:13)? Share your thoughts with your group.

Share personal prayer requests including, those regarding potential witnessing opportunities.

GROUP PRAYER TIME (10-15 minutes)

Give thanks to the Holy Spirit for his activity in your lives, especially the actions of the Spirit mentioned during the group share time.

Remember each other's personal prayer requests.

LIVE IT OUT (between meetings)
- Continue to pray for your team members.
- Pray the Word by using the Scripture themes of this session in your ongoing prayers.
- Live out the Word by *asking Holy Spirit to empower you to be a witness for Christ, to guide you into truth, and to flow out of you to other persons.*

LOOK AHEAD (before the next meeting)
- Thoughtfully read the opening comments of Session 9.
- Discover the Bible's thoughts on *co-working with Christ.*
- Think through the contribution you will make in the GROUP SHARE TIME at the next session.

PERSONAL NOTES

SESSION 9
Co-Working with Christ

When we are serving the Lord, it is all too easy to think that *we* are really doing the work and producing the results. After all, we are the closest ones to the action. It's our lips that speak, our hands that work, our minds that think. But there is One who is more involved than we are, who is closer to the action than we are. That One is Christ. The work is first of all his work. The words are his words. The love is his love. The purposes are his purposes.

Whenever and wherever we serve the Lord, we are really co-working with Christ. He leads, we follow. He initiates, we respond. We give because he first gave to us. We forgive because he first forgave us. We love because he has first loved us.

If we look back at our previous sessions, it is easy to see the co-working Christ. The *power of team* came as Christ fused our hearts and minds into one and caused us to think and work together. The *love that never fails* was his love working in us and through us. We *built each other up* because Christ's love flowed to us and through us. We *won over sin* and effectively *engaged the enemy* because "two are better than one . . . and three strands are not quickly broken" (Eccl. 4:9, 12). Our *supportive prayers* for each other released God's power and grace in our lives. We got *shaped by the Word* because Christ, who is the Word, dwells in us richly.

We'll find a similar pattern as we look to the prayer-care-share sessions ahead. We will *pray* for those in our spheres of influence, but it will be God's power that touches them. We will pray for *open doors*, but it will be the Lord who opens doors. We will see captives set free, but it will be Jesus who sets them free. We will see Christ, who is at the Father's right hand, working in us and through us to do what we ask in his name (John 14:12-14).

We will *care* for needy persons because God first cared for us and graciously met our needs. The sinners we welcome will meet the One who long ago welcomed tax collectors and sinners. We will lay down our lives for others because Christ laid down his life for us. Co-working with Christ means that we are living out his vision, in his power, for his glory.

We will *share* the gospel with those who haven't heard, looking for lost sheep with the heart of our loving Shepherd. And we will join the throng of his witnesses committed to bring the gospel to the ends of the earth, because we are empowered by the Holy Spirit (Acts 1:8).

God has always worked to equip, empower, and guide those who have served him. Abraham, called from his homeland to a strange new life, was "blessed by God to be a blessing" (Gen. 12:2). Moses, having heard the call of God to lead his people, was assured, "I will be with you" (Ex. 3:12). David, called from flocks and fields to shepherd Israel, came against the giant Goliath "in the name of the Lord Almighty" (1 Sam. 17:45). The disciples, called to be fishers of men, were prepared for that role by Jesus himself. The apostle Paul—God's co-worker to carry the gospel to the Gentiles—was first shaped for service by being "caught up to the third heaven" and later learned from a thorn in the flesh that "God's grace is sufficient and his power made perfect in weakness" (2 Cor.12:2, 9). Jesus himself co-worked with his Father. He said, "The Son can do nothing by himself; he can do only what he sees his Father doing, because whatever the Father does the Son also does (John 5:19).

Co-working with Christ will require serious effort on our part, blended with God's all-sufficient power, which is always equal to the need. To be effective in ministry, it's essential we learn the all-important lesson of co-working with Christ.

DISCOVER YOUR BIBLE

Romans 14:7-8
For none of us lives for ourselves alone, and none of us dies for ourselves alone. If we live, we live for the Lord; and if we die, we die for the Lord. So, whether we live or die, we belong to the Lord.

2 Corinthians 9:8
And God is able to bless you abundantly, so that in all things at all times, having all that you need, you will abound in every good work.

Ephesians 2:10
For we are God's handiwork, created in Christ Jesus to do good works, which God prepared in advance for us to do.

Ephesians 4:15-16
Instead, speaking the truth in love, we will grow to become in every respect the mature body of him who is the head, that is, Christ. From him the whole body, joined and held together by every supporting ligament, grows and builds itself up in love, as each part does its work.

Philippians 4:13
I can do all this through [Christ] who gives me strength.

REFLECTION (15-20 minutes)

1. According to the above verses, why were we created?

2. How does God work in us and with us to accomplish his purposes?

3. What's it like to be blessed by God "in all things, at all times" with "all that you need"? What is the fruit of all those blessings?

4. How does it make you feel to be a co-worker with Christ? How do these verses encourage you in your efforts to serve the Lord?

5. How might you increase your effectiveness as a co-worker with Christ?

GROUP SHARE TIME (20-30 minutes)
What is the most fulfilling part of co-working with Christ? If you had the time and the spiritual gifts, what would you most like to accomplish in the future with the help of Christ? Share your thoughts with your group.

Share personal requests and expressions of gratitude that others can remember in prayer.

GROUP PRAYER TIME (10-15 minutes)
Intercede for each other. Pray that each of you will be aware of the "good works" that God has prepared you to do, and will have the wisdom and ability to take up ministries as God calls.

LIVE IT OUT (between meetings)
- Continue to support each other in daily prayer. Pray for God to bless each of you abundantly.
- Pray the Word by translating the Bible verses from this session into prayers of praise, thanks, confession and intercession.
- Live out the Word by *living for the Lord, abounding in every good work for which God has created us, and speaking the truth in love.*

LOOK AHEAD (before the next meeting)
- Thoughtfully read the opening comments of Session 10.
- Discover the Bible's thoughts on *great things by prayer*.
- Think through the contribution you will make in the GROUP SHARE TIME at the next session.

PERSONAL NOTES

PART TWO: Prayer (Sessions 10-14)

This next section is about prayer--a certain kind of prayer. It's about prayer that releases God's power and grace into the lives of others. It's about life-changing prayer that opens the door for the Spirit to work and brings people into a saving relationship with Jesus Christ. One of the most important assignments a believer can have is to pray family and friends to Christ.

To pray is to co-labor with the all-powerful God, who has ordained that his power be directed into people's lives by your prayers. R. A. Torrey writes, "All that God is, and . . . has, is at the disposal of prayer. Prayer can do anything that God can do, and as God can do anything, prayer is omnipotent." This power belongs to all believers. After telling us that "the prayer of a righteous person is powerful and effective," James observes that Elijah—an Old Testament prophet who prayed with great power--was "just like us" (James 5:16-17). In other words, you and I can pray with as much power as Elijah did.

Jesus reminds his followers that if we have faith in him, we will be able to do even greater things than he did, because he has gone to the Father and stands ready to do whatever we ask in his name (John 14:12-14). In the next five sessions you will learn to pray for the kinds of things God wants to happen in the lives of people in your spheres of influence. You will learn to pray with power.

All evangelism must begin in prayer. Things will happen when we pray for the unsaved that won't happen if we don't pray. Count on it!

SESSION 10
Great Things by Prayer

No one ever prayed as Jesus did. Prayer was key to his greatness. E. M. Bounds said of Jesus' prayer life, "Prayer was the secret of his power, the law of his life, the inspiration of his toil, and the source of his wealth, his joy, his communion and his strength." Jesus prayed at every major milestone of his life: at his baptism, before calling his disciples, before being transfigured, before the Lord's Supper, before the cross, on the cross, as he died, and before he ascended. He gained victories through prayer (John 11:41-42) and averted temptation through prayer (John 6:15).

No wonder, then, that Jesus prepared his disciples to do great things in the same way. He told them, "Very truly I tell you, whoever believes in me will do the works I have been doing, and they will do even greater things than these, because I am going to the Father. And I will do whatever you ask in my name, so that the Father may be glorified in the Son. You may ask me for anything in my name, and I will do it" (John 14:12-14).

At first blush that sounds preposterous. How could the disciples possibly do the kinds of things he did? He preached brilliant sermons to huge crowds, walked on water, stilled a storm, healed the sick, raised the dead, and fed tens of thousands starting with a bag lunch. He was the Son of God; they were unschooled, ordinary men. What was he thinking?

What Jesus was thinking was that these ordinary men would do extraordinary things because he, Jesus, would be on the throne of the universe hearing and answering their prayers and acting in accord with their prayer requests. He was saying, "Prayer forges a link from earth to heaven and heaven to earth. If you use prayer to ask for the very things I want to see happen on earth, I will do them. And yes, some of the things you do will be even greater than the things I did. That is my commitment to you. That is my commitment to the Father, who will be glorified through the great things that you do."

And, they did ask! The book of Acts is filled with prayer meetings. In Acts 1:14 we are told that they "devoted themselves to prayer." A little later, together with the fellowship of believers, they once again "devoted themselves to . . . prayer" (Acts 2:42). Shortly after that when an "overlooked widows" problem surfaced they wisely appointed others to serve the widows so that they could "devote themselves to prayer and the ministry of the word" (Acts 6:4).

The proof of Jesus' pledge was not long in coming. The group of believers prayed and the promised Holy Spirit came with power. They prayed, preached a sermon, and three thousand persons repented, believed and were baptized. They prayed, and "everyone was filled with awe, and many wonders and miraculous signs were done by the apostles" (Acts 2:42-44). They continued to pray, and "the Lord added to their number daily those who were being saved." Ordered to stop speaking of Jesus, they prayed, "Now, Lord . . . enable your servants to speak your word with great boldness. Stretch out your hand to heal and perform miraculous signs and wonders" (Acts 4:29-30). And God's "yes" came with a violent shaking and a fresh filling of the Holy Spirit.

Prayer is the point at which God interacts with believers to see his will accomplished on earth. Evangelism rooted in prayer will always be effective.

Day after day the disciples recalled Jesus' pledge to answer prayers in accord with his will so they could do great things for him. They used the key of prayer to unlock some very large doors, the doors of the kingdom.

Prayer is the cornerstone of effective ministry. Nothing we do for Christ is effective without it. No human effort can take the place of God's hand moving through prayer. When God's people pray in Jesus' name, great things happen: the Spirit moves, power is unleashed, people get saved, and the church is built. And the risen, ascended, reigning Christ gets the credit. He is the one doing it.

DISCOVER YOUR BIBLE

Luke 11:5-8
Then Jesus said to them, "Suppose you have a friend, and you go to him at midnight and say, 'Friend, lend me three loaves of bread; a friend of mine on a journey has come to me, and I have no food to offer him.' And suppose the one inside answers, 'Don't bother me. The door is already locked, and my children and I are in bed. I can't get up and give you anything.' I tell you, even though he will not get up and give you the bread because of friendship, yet because of your shameless audacity he will surely get up and give you as much as you need."

John 14:12-14
"Very truly I tell you, whoever believes in me will do the works I have been doing, and they will do even greater things than these, because I am going to the Father. And I will do whatever you ask in my name, so that the Father may be glorified in the Son. You may ask me for anything in my name, and I will do it."

John 15:7-8
"If you remain in me and my words remain in you, ask whatever you wish, and it will be done for you. This is to my Father's glory, that you bear much fruit, showing yourselves to be my disciples."

Ephesians 6:18
And pray in the Spirit on all occasions with all kinds of prayers and requests. With this in mind, be alert and always keep on praying for all the Lord's people.

REFLECTION (15-20 minutes)

1. What do these passages teach us about prayer? Which of these teachings are the most exciting? Which are most challenging?

2. What are the chances that you can do even greater things than Jesus did (John 14:12-14)? What would you most like to see happen as a result of your prayers?

3. What does Jesus' going to the Father have to do with your getting answers to prayer? What does it mean to ask in Jesus name?

4. Why are ministry efforts without much prayer likely to fail? What kind of praying will it take for you to be effective in ministry?

5. How will God be glorified if your prayers are effective?

GROUP SHARE TIME (20-30 minutes)

What are some of the best things about your prayer life? How would you like to improve your prayer life? Share your thoughts with the group.

Share praises and prayer requests.

GROUP PRAYER TIME (10-15 minutes)
Pray for each person in the group. Give thanks for the good things happening in the prayer lives of fellow members. Pray for the desired improvements.

LIVE IT OUT (between meetings)
- Remember before the Lord the prayer requests of your support group friends. Pray that all may continue to grow stronger in prayer.
- Pray the Word by transposing thoughts from the passages that you have studied in this session into prayer.
- Live out the Word by *praying with shameless audacity for needy friend, praying for the fruit that will show that you are a disciple,* and *praying in the Spirit on all occasions with all kinds of prayers and requests.*

LOOK AHEAD (before the next meeting)
- Thoughtfully read the opening comments of Session 11.
- Discover the Bible's thoughts on *praying for the unsaved*.
- Begin to create a *Loving People to Jesus* list with the names of family members, friends, co-workers or neighbors who do not appear to have a personal relationship with Christ. (See appendix A.) Prepare to share this list during the group share time at your next session.

PERSONAL NOTES

SESSION 11
Pray for the Unsaved

God's Word urges us to make "requests, prayers, intercession, and thanksgiving . . . for everyone." That mandate clearly includes praying for the unsaved, for Paul goes on to link that urgent command to the truth that "God our Savior . . . wants all [persons] to be saved and to come to a knowledge of the truth." In the very next sentence, he reminds us that such prayer "is good, and pleases God our Savior" (1 Tim. 2:1-4).

All evangelism must begin in prayer. Things will happen when we pray that won't happen if we don't pray. The first thing that will happen is that *we will be changed*. I learned that in a very personal way. To be effective for God I needed to become more deeply concerned for the spiritual well-being of unsaved persons, more aware of God's heart for them. I found that the more I prayed for yet-to-be-followers of Christ, the more I cared. The more I cared, the harder I prayed. The harder I prayed, the more I wanted God's best for them and the more effective I was in reaching out to them. In that sense, prayer changed *me*.

Second, prayer will *build relationships*. Most people come to Christ because they have a relationship with a Christian who has shown them the love of Christ. Intercession builds relational bridges—bridges of love that connect us to the persons we pray for and connect them to Christ.

Third, prayer *gains access* where hearts are closed. Some people refuse to open a Bible. They may turn a blind eye to God's power in creation. They may brush off the testimony of believers and spurn the church. They may close their hearts and minds to the gospel. But they cannot keep the Spirit from moving in their hearts—the Spirit who moves when God's people pray. The unknown author of *The Kneeling Christian* said it best: "Men may spurn our appeals, reject our message, oppose our arguments, despise our persons, but they are helpless against our prayers."

How should we pray for those who are not saved? Evangelism prayer starts with *burden*. Jesus' call to pray for harvesters arose out of his shepherd's heart for harassed and helpless sheep. Paul's fervent prayer for fellow Israelites arose out of his "heart's desire . . . that they might be saved" (Rom. 10:1). Prayers without burden are lifeless and perfunctory. When Salvation Army workers reported their failure to win souls, their leader William Booth proposed a two-word solution: "Try tears." Burdened hearts love the lost. Burdened hearts weep. Burdened hearts pray fervently and powerfully. You can't produce this sense of burden on your own. But the closer you come to God's heart, the more you will sense and begin to share in his passion for those who are lost.

Praying for yet-to-be-believers also requires *perseverance*. Jesus applauded the shameless perseverance of the man who pleaded with a neighbor at midnight to give him bread for a friend (Luke 11:5-8). I am sure that Jesus also applauded the persevering prayers of George Mueller, who in 1844 began to pray daily for five individuals who did not know the Lord. One by one they came to faith as Mueller persisted in prayer. The last of the five became a Christ-follower shortly after Mueller's death, more than 63 years after he first began to pray.

Our best evangelistic prayers are going to be *Scripture prayers*. Since "no one can come to [Jesus] unless the Father . . . draws him," Scripture prayer means praying that the Father will draw them (John 6:44). Since the evil one blinds the minds of unbelievers to keep them in darkness, Scripture prayer means that we pray for the Holy Spirit to: "Open their eyes and turn them from darkness to light, and form the power of Satan to God." (Acts 26:18). Since the devil snatches away gospel seed sown in the hearts of people, Scripture prayer means praying that they will "hear the word and understand it" (Matt. 13:23).

Do you want to be used by God to reach the unsaved? Pray first that God will give you a burden and perseverance. Then go on to pray that God will draw the unsaved to himself, will cause them to hear the Word and see the light of the gospel. That kind of praying will unleash heavenly power in their hearts and lives—power infused with God's love and mighty to save. Imagine that!

DISCOVER YOUR BIBLE

Job 42:8-9
"My servant Job will pray for you, and I will accept his prayer and not deal with you according to your folly. You have not spoken the truth about me, as my servant Job has." So Eliphaz the Temanite, Bildad the Shuhite and Zophar the Naamathite did what the LORD told them; and the LORD accepted Job's prayer.

Romans 9:2-3, 10:1
I have great sorrow and unceasing anguish in my heart. For I could wish that I myself were cursed and cut off from Christ for the sake of my people, those of my own race . . . Brothers and sisters, my heart's desire and prayer to God for the Israelites is that they may be saved.

1 Timothy 2:1, 3-4
I urge, then, first of all, that petitions, prayers, intercession and thanksgiving be made for all people . . . This is good, and pleases God our Savior, who wants all people to be saved and to come to a knowledge of the truth.

2 Peter 3:9
The Lord is not slow in keeping his promise, as some understand slowness. Instead he is patient with you, not wanting anyone to perish, but everyone to come to repentance.

REFLECTION (15-20 minutes)

1. What do we learn from these passages about praying for the unsaved?

2. How does God stimulate prayer for people who can't pray for themselves (Job 42:8-9)? Who among the unsaved has God put on your list? How will he react to your prayers?

3. What made Paul pray so passionately for his unsaved countrymen (Rom. 9:2-3, 10:1)? What difference would it make if believers today felt that way about the unsaved?

4. How does God feel about unsaved persons? What might change in our actions if we felt the way God feels?

5. Knowing that a burden for the lost comes from God's heart, what steps can you take to begin to feel such a burden for the unsaved in your life?"

GROUP SHARE TIME (20-30 minutes)

Who in your spheres of influence are apart from Christ and need you to pray for their salvation? How heavy is your burden for them? [The group must keep these names confidential.]

Share your personal prayer requests and reasons you have for thanksgiving to God.

GROUP PRAYER TIME (10-15 minutes)
Cover each other in prayer, giving thanks and interceding for personal requests. Pray also that God will give you such a love and burden for those on your list that you will be able to *pray* for them faithfully, build *caring* relationships with them, and eventually *share* the gospel with them.

LIVE IT OUT (between meetings)
- Regularly ask God to make you and your fellow group members faithful and fervent intercessors. Check out *Biblical Ways to Pray for Seekers* in Appendix B. Learn the themes and Scriptures of this prayer and use them regularly as you pray for unsaved persons.
- Pray the Word--the Bible verses that you have just studied. Seek to discern and pray God's heart as revealed in these verses.
- Live out the Word *by praying for unsaved persons on your prayer-care-share list and by making "petitions, prayers, intercessions and thanksgiving . . . for all people."*

LOOK AHEAD (before the next meeting)
- Thoughtfully read the opening comments of Session 12.
- Discover the Bible's thoughts on *praying for open doors*.
- Think through the contribution you will make in the GROUP SHARE TIME at the next session.

PERSONAL NOTES

SESSION 12
Pray for Open Doors

Have you ever counted the doors in your home? I was amazed to discover that we had one hundred forty-nine doors in our home: front door, back door, side door, screen door, garage doors, closet doors, shower doors, cabinet doors, washer and dryer doors, refrigerator doors, and more. Doors, as it turns out, are an important part of our lives. Our doors allow us to come and go. They allow us privacy or exposure. They allow us to protect ourselves from intruders or welcome in guests.

There's another kind of door in our personal world: virtual doors. These allow us to shut up or open up, to let people into our lives or to keep them out. The best are doors that let Christ in to change us. The worst are doors that shut God out.

God wants to come into our lives—wants to bring his blessings, his love, his joy and his peace. He wants people to open the doors of their hearts and lives to him, and to live in fellowship with him. Jesus himself used this image in Revelation 3:20: "Here I am! I stand at the door and knock. If anyone hears my voice and opens the door, I will come in and eat with him, and he with me."

So how does God get into the lives of those who have shut him out? He urges us to pray for open doors. In response to those prayers, he sends his Spirit to open doors for the gospel. That door may be the heart of a person, or it may a door of opportunity to preach the gospel in a town or city. These kinds of things don't just happen. They can't be forced. They happen when God moves in response to prayer.

Does God still work that way today? Absolutely! Years ago our family moved to a Chicago suburb to pastor a newly planted church. I prayed persistently for an open door to share the gospel. A few months after relocating we advertised some unused furniture. Craig and Linda responded to our ad and came to check it out. They agreed to buy the furniture. Then, in the relaxed conversation that followed, Craig, learning that we were Christians, came out with a question: "You Christians talk about being born again. I have often wondered what that means?" Wow! What an open door! We followed up on on that question, and within a few months God opened the door of their hearts. Christ walked right in.

After our new church moved to another location we began to pray for a way to reach out to the community. God opened another door. Our outreach ministry started with 80-plus children from the neighborhood coming to our *Story Hour* for preschool children. Then their mothers began to attend our seeker-oriented, small-group Bible studies called *Coffee Break*. Within two and a half years over fifty of those moms came to know Jesus Christ in a personal way.

Another church seeking to reach out gathered the addresses and phone numbers of eighty homes near their church. They prayed over these homes for three months, asking God to open doors. They also gathered the addresses of a second group of eighty homes for which they did not pray during that time. After three months they phoned the people in the homes that they had prayed for and offered to come to their home to pray with them. Sixty-four said yes! They also called the eighty homes that were not prayed for with the same offer. Only one said yes. Clearly, it was prayer that opened doors.

Do you want to see doors opening for evangelism among your friends and acquaintances? Then learn from Paul, who links open doors to prayer. "Pray for us," he writes, "that God may open a door for our message" (Col. 4:3).

Pray for open doors. God will surprise you with openings you could not have imagined.

DISCOVER YOUR BIBLE

1 Corinthians 16:9
A great door for effective work has opened to me, and there are many who oppose me.

2 Corinthians 2:12
I went to Troas to preach the gospel of Christ and found that the Lord had opened a door for me.

Ephesians 6:19-20
Pray also for me, that whenever I speak, words may be given me so that I will fearlessly make known the mystery of the gospel, for which I am an ambassador in chains. Pray that I may declare it fearlessly, as I should.

Colossians 4:2-4
Devote yourselves to prayer, being watchful and thankful. And pray for us, too, that God may open a door for our message, so that we may proclaim the mystery of Christ, for which I am in chains. Pray that I may proclaim it clearly, as I should.

2 Thessalonians 3:1
As for other matters, brothers and sisters, pray for us that the message of the Lord may spread rapidly and be honored, just as it was with you.

REFLECTION (15-20 minutes)

1. What do we learn from these verses about praying for open doors? What does this teach us about effective evangelism?

2. What kinds of doors opened for Paul? What might "open doors" look like today?

3. How important was prayer in opening doors for the gospel? Do you think these would have opened if there had been no prayer?

4. Why might God choose to open and close doors based on our prayers? Why doesn't he just go ahead and do it, even if we don't ask?

5. What doors do you think Jesus would like to open for you or your church? Are you ready to pray for open doors and to walk through the ones he opens?

GROUP SHARE TIME (20-30 minutes)

What doors—service opportunities, new relationships, groups joined, casual conversations—has God opened for you in recent years? What doors for the gospel would you like God to open for you? Share your thoughts with the group.

Share personal praises and prayer requests with your group.

GROUP PRAYER TIME (10-15 minutes)

Pray prayers of thanks and intercession for each other. Pray that God will open doors of opportunity for kingdom service and help you walk through them.

LIVE IT OUT (between meetings)
- Pray for yourself and your group. *Thank* God for the opportunities he has given you to impact the lives of others for Christ.
- Pray the Word by translating the biblical truths you have studied in session 12 into prayer.
- Live out the Word by *devoting yourself to prayer, by praying and watching for open doors, and by asking God to give you words to make know the mystery of Christ.*

LOOK AHEAD (before the next meeting)
- Thoughtfully read the opening comments of Session 13.
- Discover the Bible's thoughts on *praying the Lord of harvest*.
- Prepare to comment on "harvest fields" in your GROUP SHARE TIME at the next session.

PERSONAL NOTES

SESSION 13
Pray the Lord of Harvest

Harvest times are good times. After months of dormancy, soil preparation, planting, fertilizing, watching and waiting the day finally comes. The ripe harvests are gathered into baskets or bins. The farmer celebrates his good fortune.

Jesus had an eye for harvest. Seeing crowds of people, harassed and helpless, he saw what Jewish leaders didn't see, what even his followers didn't see. He saw a ripeness for harvest. Then he said to his disciples, "The harvest is plentiful but the workers are few. Ask the Lord of the harvest, therefore, to send out workers into his harvest field" (Matthew 9:36-38).

Despite the fact that Jesus commanded us to pray for workers in the harvest, I do not often hear much praying of that sort in the church today. And frankly, I admit that for much of my life I didn't pray much for harvest workers either. I think that the problem has to do with our way of looking at things. We don't see people as Jesus sees them. We don't understand prayer as he does.

Jesus saw the crowds of people as "harassed and helpless" (Matt. 9:36), and his heart was moved with compassion. It wasn't just earthly problems like poverty, sickness, injustice, or loneliness that caused his heart to ache. He saw their hopeless spiritual condition caused by sin and Satan. He saw them as helpless to save themselves. He desperately wanted them to be brought into the kingdom and to have eternal life. I have a feeling that if we come to care for hurting and helpless people as deeply as Jesus does, we will pray vigorously for harvest workers and for ingathering of the harvest.

Jesus also assessed the harvest as "plentiful." Do we really believe that the harvest is still plentiful? It surely doesn't seem very plenteous. In many places today the harvest seems downright sparse. Many who hear the good news reject it. Others start out enthusiastic and then fall away. But Christ, who sees in ways that we do not, sees a bountiful harvest. And he commands us to pray with the assurance that there is a harvest and that harvest workers will bring it in.

Finally, Jesus understood that prayer is the means by which God will raise up a work force and release it into the harvest. To that end he charged his disciples to "ask the Lord of the harvest . . . to send out workers into his harvest field." Jesus still wants us to pray that prayer, for it is prayer that makes the harvest possible. Yes, God will choose and call and equip the workers. But he is moved to do so in response to our prayers. Jesus challenges us to pray for the harvest with the expectation that we are his co-laborers in reaping the ripened fields. If we really understand that the work force depends on our prayers, then we will surely pray with urgency.

When Jesus thought of harvest workers he probably did think of professional harvesters like missionaries, pastors, evangelists, and teachers. But I am sure that he was also thinking of ordinary believers like you and me. He called us "salt of the earth" and "the light of the world" (Matt. 5:13-14). He commanded us to "make disciples of all the nations" (Matt. 28:19). And he promised to empower us by the Spirit so that we could be his witnesses to take the gospel to the ends of the earth (Acts 1:8).

There are harvest opportunities all around us. So when we pray for harvest workers, we are praying for ourselves and for all of God's people. We are praying that we will feel what Jesus felt when he saw people who were harassed and helpless. We are praying that we will see what Jesus saw when he said, "Open your eyes and look at the fields! They are ripe for harvest" (John 4:35). We pray and then roll up our sleeves and step out into the harvest fields. That's what Jesus mandates; that's what he expects.

DISCOVER YOUR BIBLE

Matthew 9:36-38
When he saw the crowds, he had compassion on them, because they were harassed and helpless, like sheep without a shepherd. Then he said to his disciples, "The harvest is plentiful but the workers are few. Ask the Lord of the harvest, therefore, to send out workers into his harvest field."

John 4:35-38
"Don't you have a saying, 'It's still four months until harvest'? I tell you, open your eyes and look at the fields! They are ripe for harvest. Even now the one who reaps draws a wage and harvests a crop for eternal life, so that the sower and the reaper may be glad together. Thus the saying 'One sows and another reaps' is true. I sent you to reap what you have not worked for. Others have done the hard work, and you have reaped the benefits of their labor."

Acts 4:24, 29-31
When they heard [the threats of Jewish leaders] they raised their voices together in prayer to God. "Sovereign Lord," they said, "you made the heavens and the earth and the sea, and everything in them . . . . Now, Lord, consider their threats and enable your servants to speak your word with great boldness. . . . Stretch out your hand to heal and perform signs and wonders through the name of your holy servant Jesus."

After they prayed, the place where they were meeting was shaken. And they were all filled with the Holy Spirit and spoke the word of God boldly.

REFLECTION (15-20 minutes)

1. When Jesus talked about "sheep without a shepherd" and "plentiful harvests," what did he mean? If he lived in your community today, what would he see?

2. Jesus had an eye for harvest. What will it take for us to see people as Jesus saw them?

3. What role does prayer have in harvesting? Is Jesus' request still valid (Matt. 9:38)?

4. What was exceptional about the crisis prayers of the early Christians (Acts 4)? How do they compare to the typical crisis prayers you hear today?

5. What do you think would happen if millions of believers in the world today fervently prayed for harvest workers? What if your church so prayed? What if your group so prayed?

GROUP SHARE TIME (20-30 minutes)
Jesus says, "Open your eyes and look at the fields! They are ripe for harvest" (John 4:35). What kind of harvest potential do you see in your community? In your workplace? In your neighborhood? How would you evaluate your personal harvest efforts? Those of your church?

Prepare for the prayer time by sharing your blessings and your prayer requests.

GROUP PRAYER TIME (10-15 minutes)
Pray for the requests of your group's members and rejoice with them over the blessings.

Pray for the spiritual harvest in your community. Ask God to give you "harvest eyes" and to guide you and your church into harvest ministries.

LIVE IT OUT (between meetings)
- Continue to remember each other in prayers. Pray especially that God will open your eyes to the spiritual harvest around you and help you meet the needs of those whose hearts he is preparing. Continue to soak those on your Prayer-Care-Share List (Appendix A) in prayer.
- Pray the Word by praying for sheep without a shepherd, for persecuted Christians, and for persons who are ready to come to Christ.
- Live out the Word by *watching for ripe fruit, by sowing and reaping, and by being prepared to speak the Word with boldness when given the opportunity.*

LOOK AHEAD (before the next meeting)
- Thoughtfully read the opening comments of Session 14.
- Discover the Bible's thoughts on *setting captives free*.
- Think through the contribution you will make in the GROUP SHARE TIME at the next session about "enemy" activities you are aware of.

PERSONAL NOTES

SESSION 14
Setting Captives Free

There are two powerful forces at work in the world today—the power of God and the power of Satan. Satan, bent on thwarting God's plan of salvation, goes about "like a roaring lion looking for someone to devour" (1 Peter 5:8). Christ, the Son of God, intent on saving the world, goes to the cross so that "the prince of this world will be driven out" (John 12:31).

Though God's power is infinitely greater than Satan's, Satan still has the capacity to disrupt our efforts and diminish our effectiveness. Any time you seek to reach someone for Christ you are entering enemy territory. If you are intent on seeing captives set free, be prepared to face some real spiritual warfare. Do not face the enemy in your own strength. That would be folly and a sure pathway to defeat. Prayer is the power by which we are equipped to overcome the evil one. Prayer is our supreme weapon in setting captives free.

The apostle John observes that into the lives of the unsaved, loosening Satan's enslaving grip on their lives.

How should we pray against the work of the devil? First, pray *protection* for yourself. The devil will not take your meddling in his world sitting down. He will do everything possible to foil your efforts, even to the point of a personal attack. Jesus, understanding the danger of the devil's attacks and our need for protection, urged us to pray, "Father . . . deliver us from the evil one" (Matt. 6:13). You can be sure that the Father will hear and answer when you pray that prayer.

Second, ask the Spirit to help you *discern* the devil's strongholds in the lives of those you are trying to reach. Is he enslaving people in addictions, materialism, bitterness, pornography, depression or pride? Pray in specific ways for the Lord's intervention. Use the God-given weapons that "have divine power to demolish strongholds." God's mighty weapons--prayer, faith, hope, love, God's Word--are effective in demolishing arguments and pretensions that set themselves up against the knowledge of God (2 Cor. 10:4-5).

Third, *use the Word*. The Word is the "sword of the Spirit" (Eph. 6:17). It is alive and active (Heb. 4:12) and is "the power of God that brings salvation to everyone who believes (Rom. 1:16). The devil is no match for the Word. When tempted by Satan in the wilderness Jesus negated every temptation with a word from Scripture (Matt. 4:1-11). As you use the Word, pray that it will do its work. Pray that the devil will not succeed in snatching it away before it yields its harvest (Luke 8:12).

The devil dreads our prayers more than anything else. A mighty prayer warrior once said, "Do you realize that there is nothing the devil dreads so much as prayer? His great concern is to keep us from praying. He loves to see us 'up to our eyes' in work—provided we do not pray. He does not fear if we are eager Bible students—provided we are little in prayer. Oswald Chambers wisely said: "The prayer of the feeblest saint who lives in the Spirit and keeps right with God is a terror to Satan. The very powers of darkness are paralyzed by prayer. No wonder Satan tries to keep our minds fussy in active work till we cannot think in prayer."

Satan trembles when we pray. By means of prayer, the power of the omnipotent God of heaven and earth is brought against him. When God moves in response to our prayers the devil doesn't stand a chance. By prayer, the kingdom of God is built, and by prayer, the kingdom of Satan is destroyed. Where there is much prayer in Jesus' name, the work of Satan is undone and captives are set free. Where there is little or no prayer, captives remain enslaved. Christ, who defeated Satan once and for all on the cross, continues to enforce his victory through our prayers.

DISCOVER YOUR BIBLE

Isaiah 61:1-3
The Spirit of the Sovereign LORD is on me, because the LORD has anointed me to proclaim good news to the poor. He has sent me to bind up the brokenhearted, to proclaim freedom for the captives and release from darkness for the prisoners, to proclaim the year of the LORD's favor and the day of vengeance of our God, to comfort all who mourn, and provide for those who grieve in Zion—to bestow on them a crown of beauty instead of ashes, the oil of joy instead of mourning, and a garment of praise instead of a spirit of despair.

John 17:11, 15
"Holy Father, protect them by the power of your name, the name you gave me, so that they may be one as we are one. . ... My prayer is not that you take them out of the world but that you protect them from the evil one."

2 Corinthians 4:4
The god of this age has blinded the minds of unbelievers, so that they cannot see the light of the gospel that displays the glory of Christ, who is the image of God.

2 Corinthians 10:4-5
The weapons we fight with are not the weapons of the world. On the contrary, they have divine power to demolish strongholds. We demolish arguments and every pretension that sets itself up against the knowledge of God, and we take captive every thought to make it obedient to Christ.

REFLECTION (15-20 minutes)

1. What, according to Isaiah's prophecy, would Jesus do (see Lk.4:18-19) to set captives free (Isaiah 61:1-3)?

2. What do these verses reveal about Jesus awareness of the devil? What difference would it make if we were more aware of the evil one?

3. How does the devil try to keep people from knowing Christ? What difference can prayer make?

4. What strongholds in the lives of your non-Christian friends and acquaintances would you like to see demolished? What can you do help make this happen?

5. Why do you think the devil dreads our prayers? What tactics might he employ to keep us from praying?

GROUP SHARE TIME (20-30 minutes)

According to 1 John 5:19 the whole world "is under the control of the evil one." Share with your group how you see the enemy attempting to frustrate God's redemptive plan in your community. How might he be using media, busy schedules, sports, entertainment, materialism, worldliness, promiscuity and the like to hold his "captives?" What can you do to upset his plans?

Share your personal joys and concerns with your group.

GROUP PRAYER TIME (10-15 minutes)

Pray for the personal needs of each member of your group. Also, pray that you, your family members, and your friends in Christ may be delivered from the evil one (Matt. 6:13). Make use of the Bible verses just studied to pray for spiritual captives.

LIVE IT OUT (between meetings)

Pray over the joys and concerns of your fellow group members and ask that God will protect each of you from the evil one.

Pray the Word using the following warfare prayer prompts:
- *Praise* God who is willing and able to destroy the works of the devil and to protect his children.
- *Ask* Jesus to teach you how to make use of prayer as a weapon to defeat Satan and to help advance the kingdom of God.
- *Intercede* for believer you know who are under attack by the evil one.
- *Pray* for persons who do not know Christ and ask God to set them free from the powers of evil.

LOOK AHEAD (before the next meeting)
- Thoughtfully read the opening comments of Session 15.
- Discover the Bible's thoughts on *a lifestyle of love.*
- Think through the contribution you will make about costly love commitments you have made at your next GROUP SHARE TIME.

PERSONAL NOTES

PART THREE: Care (Sessions 15-20)

In the *Prayer* section, you learned that you can co-labor with God by means of prayer, releasing power and grace into people's lives. Now in the *Care* section, you will learn that caring is another way to cooperate with what God is doing in the world. By caring you become a channel of God's love into people's lives.

As believers, we know that God loves us. God also loves those who are not yet believers. To be effective channels of his love to others, we need to be fully aware of how much God loves them. They may be far away from him, as the prodigal son was from his father (Luke 15:11-32). But our Father, like that of the prodigal son, still thinks of them as his children and longs to see them come home. They don't know that, but you do. Because you have a relationship with some of these wayward ones, you are well positioned to be a channel of God's love to them. Reach out with a love like that of Jesus, who "welcomed sinners and ate with them" (Luke 15:2). People will be drawn to the love of Christ by experiencing his love through you.

As you reach out to others in love you will not only be *like* Christ, you will be ministering *to* Christ. You can expect Jesus to say to you, "Come take your inheritance, the kingdom prepared for you from the creation of the world," because whatever you did for the least of these--the hungry. . . the thirsty. . . a stranger . . . those needing clothes . . . those sick or those in prison--"you did for me" (Matt. 25:34-40). What you do out of love for others, you do for Christ.

SESSION 15

A Lifestyle of Love

A lifestyle is a way of life shaped by our decisions. The lifestyle you choose is critical; it affects your thinking, actions, values, relationships. It dictates where you spend your time, energies, and money. One popular lifestyle is materialism: deciding to make as much money as you can, to live in the biggest house you can afford, to buy things that show your wealth and status. But there are other options. Choosing a lifestyle of love for your neighbors, for example, will make love the determinative factor in your life.

Love is what God expects of us. John emphasized that "if we love one another, God lives in us and his love is made complete in us" (1 John 4:12). As God's love in Christ broke through in the early church, it created a love so radically different that a new word had to be created: *agape.*

Agape love can be defined as a *costly commitment, in Jesus' name, for the well-being of others*. This definition has four basic elements that capture the biblical concept of love. First, love is a commitment that believers make *in Jesus' name*. Jesus is the model for our love. We are called to "live a life of love, just as Christ loved us and gave himself up for us as a fragrant offering and sacrifice to God" (Eph. 5:2). Christ is the source of our love, and lives out his love-life today in us and through us. It is his love that is shed abroad in our hearts and poured out through us for others. Without Christ in our hearts, we cannot love as we ought to love. With him abiding in us, we cannot help but love.

Second, love is a *costly commitment*. It will cost us much: time, energy, careful communication, active listening, empathy, and transparency. It will require sensitivity to people and involvement in their life issues. It may even mean suffering, sacrifice or loss. It's a love that makes a person willing to "lay down his life for his friends" (John 15:13) and to love enemies (Matt. 5:44). Love is willing to pay the price because it has made a commitment rooted in Christ's love and mandate.

Third, love is for *others*—our neighbors: family members, friends, fellow believers, coworkers, and those who live on our street. To fulfill the love mandate we need "people eyes": eyes that see the needs in others' lives. We need ears that hear the pain and hurt in people's words. We need hands ready to help others. We need feet that will move us toward another person and their need. Our minds need to be focused on others rather than on self.

Finally, our love commitment is for the *well-being* of others. Love lifts. Love blesses. Love seeks the best for the other person. It always acts with the best interests of the others in mind. Love is a delivery system, bringing God's life-changing love to people in need. Paul reminded us that love "always protects, always trust, always hopes, always perseveres. Love never fails" (1 Cor. 13:7-8).

God the Father made the costly commitment of sending his Son to die for us. Christ made the costliest commitment ever known to humankind by his agonizing death on the cross. We now are challenged to make a self-sacrificial commitment by giving ourselves for others. No one needs our commitment more than the lost people around us. Dr. Bob Smith, a godly professor at Bethel College in St. Paul, Minnesota, once remarked, "Ninety percent of evangelism is love." Are you willing to make a love commitment for the unsaved ones you know? There is a power in that kind of love. It's a power that flows from God, leading others to Christ. A lifestyle of love is a life worth living—for God's sake and for the many who have yet to know the full extent of his love.

DISCOVER YOUR BIBLE

John 13:34-35
"A new command I give you: Love one another. As I have loved you, so you must love one another. By this everyone will know that you are my disciples, if you love one another."

Romans 13:8-9
Let no debt remain outstanding, except the continuing debt to love one another, for whoever loves others has fulfilled the law. The commandments, "You shall not commit adultery," "You shall not murder," "You shall not steal," "You shall not covet," and whatever other command there may be, are summed up in this one command: "Love your neighbor as yourself."

1 Corinthians 13:4-8
Love is patient, love is kind. It does not envy, it does not boast, it is not proud. It does not dishonor others, it is not self-seeking, it is not easily angered, it keeps no record of wrongs. Love does not delight in evil but rejoices with the truth. It always protects, always trusts, always hopes, always perseveres. Love never fails.

1 John 4:19, 21
We love because he first loved us. . . . And he has given us this command: Anyone who loves God must also love their brother and sister.

REFLECTION (15-20 minutes)

1. Think of some outstanding acts of love from Jesus' life. How did those acts affect those he loved?

2. What will people know if believers truly love each other? What will they conclude if we don't? Why should we care about what people think?

3. What is Paul implying by calling love a debt? How do we go about paying off this debt? Can it ever be fully paid off? (See Rom. 13:8-9.)

4. In 1 Corinthians 13:4-8 there are eight negative phrases that describe what love is not. What words would you use to describe the opposite of each of these?

5. What will love actually look like for you at home, at work, in the church, among your friends and acquaintances? Be as specific as possible.

GROUP SHARE TIME (20-30 minutes)

Share with each other stories of costly love commitments that you have made or are making for other people. What did these commitments cost you? How did those you loved benefit?

Share personal blessings and concerns in preparation for the prayer time.

GROUP PRAYER TIME (10-15 minutes)

Pray for the personal joys and concerns of each member. Pray also that God will give you love opportunities like those in Jesus' life, causing those who experience his love through you to become more open to Christ.

LIVE IT OUT (between meetings)

- Continue to pray for fellow group members every day. Pray for and expect new love opportunities for yourself and the others.
- <u>Pray the Word</u>. Find reasons for *praise, thanksgiving, confession, petition* and *intercession* in these verses.
- <u>Live out the Word</u> this week by *living a lifestyle of love*.

PREPARE (before the next meeting)

- Thoughtfully read the opening comments of Session 16.
- Discover the Bible's thoughts on being *called to serve*.
- In preparation for the next GROUP SHARE TIME recall some ways that you have given yourself to serve others.

PERSONAL NOTES

SESSION 16

Called to Serve

We live in a hurting world. Surveys tell us that 18,000 children die of starvation each day, 800 million people are destitute, and 10 million are refugees with no place to call home. In the United States alone, 13.5 million people are physically disabled, 7 million are mentally disabled, 7 million are alcoholics, and over one and a half million are in prison. Add to this the physically abused, sexually molested, the battered spouses, victims of crime, the incurably ill, the permanently injured, the desperate teenagers, lonely and forgotten senior citizens—and it all adds up to a deeply hurting world. This is our world--the world in which we are called to serve.

Who cares about all these hurting people? Jesus does. So do believers who have the love of Christ in their hearts. The gospels are full of Jesus' admonitions to serve people with needs. He calls us to "give to the needy" (Matt. 6:3) and to give "a cup of cold water in my name" (Mk.9:41). He commends those who feed the hungry, welcome the stranger, clothe the naked, look after the sick, and visit those in prison, affirming that such acts are really done to him (Matt. 25:34-36). We are most like him when we serve (Matt. 20:26-28).

What does it mean to serve? It means meeting another's needs, doing good without expecting anything in return. As believers, we meet needs because Christ has graciously met ours. We've been saved to serve. Like Abraham, we are "blessed to be a blessing." Our service brings hope to a hurting world and glory to God's name.

So how do we serve him in our world today? First, we *give ourselves to God* and invite him to use what he has given us. We give him the use of our eyes, our lips, our hands and our feet—every part of us. We give him our time, talents, and spiritual gifts. We give him our hearts and lives. Our service is for his glory and the building of his kingdom.

Second, *we give ourselves to people*. We are sensitive to others and their needs. We make ourselves available. Look around your home, workplace, circle of friends, or neighborhood. What needs can you meet there? Ask sincere questions that invite people to talk about their lives. Take the time to really listen. Let them know that you hear them, that you really care. Speak a kind word or send a message with a smile or a gesture. Communicate God's love by actions before you try to verbalize the good news. Small or large, whatever you do to serve others is important to God.

Third, *we meet people at their point of felt need*. As Jesus walked the paths of Palestine, many came to him with felt needs. As he reached out in love to meet their immediate needs, doors often opened for him to meet deeper needs. It still works that way today. The door opens widest at the point of greatest need, and that door is the one most likely to open to the deepest of all needs—the need to know Christ.

As servants of Christ, we have an important role in the world. Our relationships can have redeeming value, especially for those who do not know Christ. The love we show them will open them to the love of Christ. The grace we extend will prepare them to understand and accept Christ's. The forgiveness we offer will help them receive the forgiveness Christ offers. Our helping hand may turn out to be for them the helping hand of Christ.

Look around! Do you see hurting people along the roads you travel? Ask God to open your eyes to their immediate needs and their deeper needs. Ask him to help you serve them well. You can be sure he will. He is the expert! He is always willing to help one of his servants to serve well.

DISCOVER YOUR BIBLE

Matthew 20:27-28
"Whoever wants to become great among you must be your servant, and whoever wants to be first must be your slave—just as the Son of Man did not come to be served, but to serve, and to give his life as a ransom for many."

Matthew 25:34-36
"Then the King will say to those on his right, 'Come, you who are blessed by my Father; take your inheritance, the kingdom prepared for you since the creation of the world. For I was hungry and you gave me something to eat, I was thirsty and you gave me something to drink, I was a stranger and you invited me in, I needed clothes and you clothed me, I was sick and you looked after me, I was in prison and you came to visit me.'"

Galatians 5:13
You, my brothers and sisters, were called to be free. But do not use your freedom to indulge the flesh; rather, serve one another humbly in love.

1 Peter 4:11
If anyone serves, they should do so with the strength God provides, so that in all things God may be praised through Jesus Christ. To him be the glory and the power forever and ever.

REFLECTION (15-20 minutes)

1. What does it take for a prosperous Christian to become a servant? What does the greatness Jesus referred to look like today (Matt. 20:26-28)?

2. Whose needs might you, a servant of the King, be able to meet this week? What blessing does the King promise in return (Matt. 25:34-36)?

3. What would you notice if you saw a person serving others "humbly in love"? Who has modeled this kind of humble service for you?

4. The Bible says that God will provide strength for a person who serves. Why is this important? How do we acquire the strength that God offers?

5. What is the most important incentive that you have to serve?

GROUP SHARE TIME (20-30 minutes)

Share a couple of your experiences in giving of yourself to serve others. What needs did you meet? What, if anything, could you do to improve your "serve"?

Give your group members some suggestions on how they can pray for you this week.

GROUP PRAYER TIME (10-15 minutes)

Pray for the life and ministry activities of each person in your group. Thank God for the way that he has served you through his Son and his Spirit. Ask God to provide you with the strength to serve well.

LIVE IT OUT (between meetings)
- Pray for yourself and the other group members each day, asking the Lord to help you serve others well.
- Pray the Word that you have studied in this session, *asking* God for a spirit of servanthood and humility and *thanking* him for the inheritance he promises you.
- Live out the Word this week by *serving others humbly in love just as the Son of Man did, and by serving in the strength that God provides.*

PREPARE (before the next meeting)
- Thoughtfully read the opening comments of Session 17.
- Discover the Bible's thoughts on *making friends for Christ.*
- Think through the contribution you will make in the GROUP SHARE TIME at the next session.

PERSONAL NOTES

SESSION 17

Make Friends for Christ

It was years ago that I first heard of an e-mail system called Constant Contact. I liked the name and the idea from the start. This system promised limitless opportunities to get a message in front of people, and you didn't have to be an expert to use it. It wasn't long before I was regularly receiving and sending messages by way of Constant Contact.

Long before Constant Contact started up in 1995, Jesus had a way of making constant contact. He simply connected with the people he met along the pathways of life. Some were diseased, some disabled, and some demon-possessed. There were down-and-outers and up-and-outers. There were outcasts and sinners. Some he helped on the spot; others became friends and followers. He touched their lives in a way that brought love and healing. They got the message: "Somebody cares!"

Through his life Jesus was sending us a message: "If you are going to impact lives for me, you have to make contact. You have to care enough to get next to people, to earn their trust and become friends. Then you'll have a chance to share the good news."

Who are the ones we befriend? Most likely they are people we already know, people who trust us. They know us well enough to be open to friendship. Christ's love in us will serve as a magnet to draw them to us and to him. It will impel us to be involved in their lives.

Several things will help us make friends for Christ. First, we have to *spend time* with people, time that allows for meaningful, ongoing contact; time that allows us to be involved in their lives. Friends will best be able to sense our love, and Christ's love, through relaxed personal contact. Take time to find common ground with those who are not yet part of the family of God.

Next, we need to *talk with them*. Conversation is the primary way that we build bridges to our neighbors. This doesn't have to be talk about spiritual matters. More than likely it will be about the normal issues of life—work, children, schools, recreation, travel, politics—all of which can trigger opportunities for you to demonstrate caring concern. Some of these conversations will provide openings for you to speak of your source of strength and hope—Christ.

Finally, to be a friend you have to *listen*. The first duty of love is to listen. Listen with an interest in the other person. Find out what life is really like for them. Listen to their stories—what they dream about, what is going well, what needs work. People love to tell their stories. The more you know of their story, the better you will know how Christ can meet the deeper needs of their lives. It may also open the door for you to tell your story—the story of a life in union with Christ.

God's way of reaching people is *through* people like you and me. Those outside the faith are first attracted to Christians, then to Christ. The closer the contact, the deeper the friendship; and the deeper the friendship, the greater the opportunity. This doesn't mean that the friendships we build for Christ are simply evangelist projects. All true friendships are rooted in love—authentic and ongoing love.

Our neighbors—those we befriend for Christ's sake—are of inestimable value. They matter to God. They are precious to Christ. And if they are so dear to God, then you and I need to treat them with love and respect. Whatever time, energy, or effort it may take to befriend them is but a small price to pay. You just may be the one person in someone's life who reminds them there is a God who loves them and who invites them to come to him. You may be the person through whom God changes a life forever. What could be more exciting than that?

DISCOVER YOUR BIBLE

Luke 14:12-14
Then Jesus said to his host, "When you give a luncheon or dinner, do not invite your friends, your brothers or sisters, your relatives, or your rich neighbors; if you do, they may invite you back and so you will be repaid. But when you give a banquet, invite the poor, the crippled, the lame, the blind, and you will be blessed. Although they cannot repay you, you will be repaid at the resurrection of the righteous."

Luke 15:1-2
Now the tax collectors and sinners were all gathering around to hear Jesus. But the Pharisees and the teachers of the law muttered, "This man welcomes sinners and eats with them."

Luke 19:1-6 [See Luke 19:1-10 for the whole story.]
Jesus entered Jericho and was passing through. A man was there by the name of Zacchaeus; he was a chief tax collector and was wealthy. He wanted to see who Jesus was, but because he was short he could not see over the crowd. So he ran ahead and climbed a sycamore-fig tree to see him, since Jesus was coming that way. When Jesus reached the spot, he looked up and said to him, "Zacchaeus, come down immediately. I must stay at your house today." So he came down at once and welcomed him gladly.

Romans 12:14-16
Rejoice with those who rejoice; mourn with those who mourn. Live in harmony with one another. Do not be proud, but be willing to associate with people of low position.

REFLECTION (15-20 minutes)

1. What major social problem were Jesus and Paul addressing in the passages above? What was their solution?

2. How does Jesus feel about people of low position? What kept the Pharisees and teachers of the law from relating to people the way Jesus did? What's the lesson for us?

3. Who will benefit if we live out the relational lifestyle that Jesus commands?

4. What issues come to play when we befriend the poor? People of low position? Those with sinful lifestyles?

5. What might keep us from thinking of people as precious to God? What would encourage us to think of people that way?

GROUP SHARE TIME (20-30 minutes)

Who do you know that God might want you to befriend for his sake? What concrete steps could you take to make the connection? What might it cost you?

Share some reasons for thanks and your prayer concerns.

GROUP PRAYER TIME (10-15 minutes)
Share a mutual prayer time in which you pray for each other's concerns. Ask God to give you a passion for those who don't know Christ. Pray by name for friends and acquaintances who are spiritually disconnected, and invite God to show you opportunities to build new friendship in the future.

LIVE IT OUT (between meetings)
- Continue in prayer for the members of your group.
- Pray the Word by reflecting on the patterns of Jesus' life described in the Bible passages, and thinking about how they might translate into life patterns today.
- Try to live out the Word by *being aware of and trying to connect with people who are not now in your circle of friends.*

PREPARE (before the next meeting)
- Thoughtfully read the opening comments of Session 18.
- Discover the Bible's thoughts on *letting your light shine.*
- Think about ways that light shines out of your life in preparation for sharing at the next GROUP SHARE TIME.

PERSONAL NOTES

SESSION 18

Let Your Light Shine

When Jesus says to us, "You are the light of the world," he pays us a huge compliment. Light is the very nature of God: "God is light; in him there is no darkness at all" (1 John 1:5). Jesus declares that he is "the light of the world" (John 8:12). To be light is to have a God-like beauty. It is to shine with the character of Christ. When Jesus calls his followers "light" he is saying, "You are beautiful, you are glorious, you are like me."

By calling us the light *of the world*, Jesus was saying, "You are absolutely crucial to life in the world." There is a darkness enshrouding humanity—a darkness of ignorance, moral decay, and gloom—that needs to be penetrated by the light of Christ. Where Christ is not known, where his light is not seen in the lives of believers, there is no light. Believers are in the world to reveal the light of Christ to the world. We are the radiance of his presence.

To help us understand the importance of our role, Jesus asks us to imagine a house—a typical Bible-times one-room house. When darkness falls all activity stops unless there is a candle or lantern. Without light there will be no more work, no more fellowship, no eating, and no more of the usual family activities. So a lamp is placed in the middle of the room. By its light, normal activities can go on. The light of our good deeds, says Jesus, have a similar effect. They make life possible in an otherwise dark world and bring people to the point of "glorifying the Father in heaven" (Matt. 5:14-16).

Archibald Campbell, a long-time missionary to Korea, wrote about the impact of Christianity in Korea. He compared life in Korea before the gospel came, with life after the Word of God had touched millions of lives and Christianity took root. Before missionaries came, Korea was a very dark place. Wife beating was commonplace. Fathers sold their daughters or wives into prostitution without qualm of conscience. Selfishness was rampant. Hospital service was almost non-existent. The lower caste were outcasts. "Men loved darkness" (John 3:19). After the gospel of God's grace took hold, within the space of two generations the country experienced a new reality—a new brightness. The light of Christ began to shine in a small percentage of the vast population. Darkness was dispelled and light began to shine into every aspect of life.

So how do believers shine? Paul tells us that their light consists "in all goodness, righteousness and truth" (Eph. 5:9). In another letter Paul says that believers are to "do everything without grumbling or arguing, so that they become blameless and pure and…shine…like stars in the universe" (Phil. 2:14-15). We make a difference for Christ not simply by our words—important as they are—but also by our lives. Letting our light shine may be as simple as a smile, a greeting or a handshake. It may involve asking a question, listening carefully, or saying thanks. It may happen as we mail a card, make a phone call or send a text. But happen it must! "Live as children of light" (Eph. 5:8).

It's wonderful and heartening to hear Jesus, the wisest man who ever lived, tag us as "the light of the world." But even as you take delight in that thought, remember that you are not "light" in and of yourself. It's only as Christ lives in you and shines through you that you are able to shine at all. And truth be told, with Christ living in you, it's impossible not to shine. Never forget that you have been "rescued from the dominion of darkness" (Col. 1:13) and brought into the kingdom of light. At the end of each day, credit Christ with every glimmer of light that streamed from you that day.

DISCOVER YOUR BIBLE

Daniel 12:3
"Those who are wise will shine like the brightness of the heavens, and those who lead many to righteousness, like the stars forever and ever."

Matthew 5:14-16
"You are the light of the world. A town built on a hill cannot be hidden. Neither do people light a lamp and put it under a bowl. Instead, they put it on its stand, and it gives light to everyone in the house. In the same way, let your light shine before others, that they may see your good deeds and glorify your Father in heaven."

Acts 13:47-48
"For this is what the Lord has commanded us: 'I have made you a light for the Gentiles, that you may bring salvation to the ends of the earth.'" When the Gentiles heard this, they were glad and honored the word of the Lord; and all who were appointed for eternal life believed.

Ephesians 5:8-9
For you were once darkness, but now you are light in the Lord. Live as children of light (for the fruit of the light consists in all goodness, righteousness, and truth).

Philippians 2:14-15
Do everything without grumbling or arguing, so that you may become blameless and pure, children of God without fault in a warped and crooked generation. Then you will shine among them like stars in the sky.

REFLECTION (15-20 minutes)

1. What is so important about light? What happens when there is no light? What is God's solution to the darkness in this world?

2. What are the real-life qualities that light represents?

3. What are the world's standards for being a bright light? How do they differ from the Bible's standards?

4. What do the phrases "shine like the brightness of the heavens" and shine "like the stars forever and ever" imply?

5. Where in your world do you see darkness? What can you do to help dispel it?

GROUP SHARE TIME (20-30 minutes)

Think about when, where, and how the light of Christ shines out of your life. Are some of the places where you shine quite dark? How could you shine even more brightly? Share your thoughts with your group.

Share some of your present reasons for gratitude and your prayer requests.

GROUP PRAYER TIME (10-15 minutes)

Share a prayer time together in which you
- *praise* Jesus Christ, the Light of the world.
- *thank* him for shining in you and through you to others.
- *ask* for Christ's light to shine ever more brightly through you so that those who now walk in darkness may come to see the light.
- *bathe* each other in blessings through your prayers of intercession.

LIVE IT OUT (between meetings)
- Continue to pray for each other and for the way God wants to use you to brighten your world.
- Pray the Word that you studied for this session. You'll find some very good reasons to give *thanks*, and also some reasons to *ask* for God's help.
- Live out the Word by *living as children of light, letting your light shine before others, and being blameless and pure.* Be especially concerned for those who live in darkness.

PREPARE (before the next meeting)
- Thoughtfully read the opening comments of Session 19.
- Discover the Bible's thoughts on *being wise toward outsiders.*
- If you can think of a time when you were wise toward an outsider be prepared to share that at your next session.

PERSONAL NOTES

SESSION 19
Be Wise Toward Outsiders

Wisdom has been defined as *the ability to live life God's way*. Jesus demonstrated that perfectly. He showed us, for example, what it means to "be wise toward outsiders" (Col. 4:5) in the comfortable way he related to persons outside of the faith. He dined with sinners, attended parties, reached out to prostitutes, touched lepers, welcomed children, crossed gender boundaries, accepted foreigners, and tactfully reproached his adversaries. Jesus was a people-person who modeled a sinner-friendly lifestyle without compromising his personal holiness. As Jesus reached out to people, outsiders became insiders.

Jesus' interpersonal style reminds us to be alert to the relational opportunities that life brings our way. His example encourages us to take the initiative, to listen carefully, to build relational bridges, and to be available to those God puts in our path. Being wise toward outsiders is a way of reaching people for Christ, a way that may depend not so much on our ability as on our availability.

For Paul, being "wise in the way you act toward outsiders" meant a *carefully conceived message*: "Let your conversation be always full of grace, seasoned with salt" (Col. 4:5-6). A study of one thousand churches done by the Willow Creek Association revealed that "having spiritual conversations with seekers is the most effective strategy for personal evangelism."

The message we send is usually more than words. Albert Mehrabian, in his book *Silent Messages*, explains that words, though important, represent only 7 percent of the messages we send. In fact, 38 percent of our messages are conveyed by the tone of our voice, and 55 percent are communicated in the nonverbal language of facial expression, gestures, eye contact, posture, dress, touching, physical nearness, and other actions.[1] A conversation that is "full of grace" will surely communicate the love of Christ in words, but much of the message will be conveyed in tone of voice and nonverbal language.

Paul also realized that to be "wise toward outsiders" was *to be adaptable*. To "win the weak," he adapted to the point of "being different things to different people" (1 Cor. 9:22). He made an effort "to please everyone in all that I do, not thinking of my own good, but of the good of all, so that they might be saved" (1 Cor. 10:33, TEV). Paul teaches that to win the lost we have to be flexible. People who do not read the Bible or listen to sermons will "read" us, and "hear" the truth through our lives. They will be attracted to Christ or repelled, depending on our actions. In other words, we can win or repulse outsiders, based on how we act toward them.

Being wise toward outsiders also means *valuing others highly*. "Value others above yourselves," says Paul, "not looking to your own interests but each of you to the interests of the others" (Phil. 2:3-4). To love others is to seek their best interests. Sometimes this conflicts with our best interests. When that happens, Paul advises, choose the interests of the other person above your own.

Faith sharing is not a one-size-fits-all formula, a canned package, or a quick-fix presentation. Faith sharing starts with a relationship in which you care so deeply for another person that it affects the way you think, the way you act, and the way you relate to them and their needs. True caring is the gateway to faith sharing. It's caring about the total life of the person to whom you witness—their life here and their life beyond the grave. That's a lot of caring. That kind of caring is only possible because of the One who cared so much for you.

[1] Albert Mehrabian, *Silent Messages,* (Wadsworth Publishing, 1971), pp. 42-44.

DISCOVER YOUR BIBLE

Acts 17:19-20, 22-23

Then they took [Paul] and brought him to a meeting of the Areopagus, where they said to him, "May we know what this new teaching is that you are presenting? You are bringing some strange ideas to our ears, and we would like to know what they mean."

Paul then stood up in the meeting of the Areopagus and said: "People of Athens! I see that in every way you are very religious. For as I walked around and looked carefully at your objects of worship, I even found an altar with this inscription: TO AN UNKNOWN GOD. So you are ignorant of the very thing you worship—and this is what I am going to proclaim to you."

1 Corinthians 9:22

To the weak I became weak, to win the weak. I have become all things to all people so that by all possible means I might save some.

1 Corinthians 10:33

I try to please everyone in every way. For I am not seeking my own good but the good of many, so that they may be saved.

Philippians 2:3-4

Do nothing out of selfish ambition or vain conceit. Rather, in humility value others above yourselves, not looking to your own interests but each of you to the interests of the others.

Colossians 4:5-6

Be wise in the way you act toward outsiders; make the most of every opportunity. Let your conversation be always full of grace, seasoned with salt, so that you may know how to answer everyone.

REFLECTION (15-20 minutes)

1. What was Paul's main concern when relating to those outside the faith?

2. What does it mean to be wise toward outsiders? What was wise about Paul's approach? What will it take for you?

3. When relating to people you do not know well, how often do you wonder where they are in their faith? Why is this important?

4. How does humility affect our way of relating to others? What are some things you might think or do if you value others above yourself?

5. When relating to outsiders, how can you "make the most of every opportunity" and to season your conversations with salt?

GROUP SHARE TIME (20-30 minutes)
Share an experience from your past in which you were wise in the way you acted toward an outsider—or *not* so wise.

Give to your teammates some reasons to rejoice with you and some things to pray for you.

GROUP PRAYER TIME (10-15 minutes)
Give God thanks for blessings and continue to intercede for each other.

Confess those times when you did not "make the most of every opportunity." Pray for the grace to "become all things to all people so that by all possible means you might save some" (1 Cor. 9:22). Ask God to open doors of opportunity for each of you in the weeks ahead.

LIVE IT OUT (between meetings)
- Continue to uphold each other in prayer. Pray that members may develop new relationships with outsiders and make the most of these opportunities.
- <u>Pray the Word</u> by turning this week's Bible verses into prayers of confession, petition and intercession.
- <u>Try to live out God's Word</u> *by valuing others above yourself and by making the most of opportunities to be wise toward outsiders.* Identify outsiders toward whom you can "be wise."

LOOK AHEAD (before the next meeting)
- Thoughtfully read the opening comments of Session 20,
- Discover the Bible's thoughts on *be quick to listen.*
- Recall the elements of a good conversational exchange you recently had as preparation for the next GROUP SHARE TIME.

PERSONAL NOTES

SESSION 20
Be Quick to Listen

I recently received a newsletter from our local *Lighthouse Mission* in which the director answered a question that he often gets: "How can I help panhandlers?" His answer surprised me. He said, "Slow down. Get to know them... and don't give them any money. People don't become homeless because they've run out of money; they become homeless because they have run out of relationships." He went on to say that "the purest (and rarest) form of generosity you can offer is your attention" (Hans Erchinger-Davis, *The Mission Beacon*, July 2017).

This director may have been speaking about a larger segment of the population than he knew. In calling attention to the primary cause for homelessness, he was pinpointing a much bigger problem in society--the problem of loneliness. It's a problem that is clearly getting worse despite the fact that we now live in a world flooded with social media.

James steps into the vacuous world of loneliness with a simple but profound suggestion: "Be quick to listen" (James 1:19). Listening is a powerful way to connect with people. It's really a form of love. We can't truly love our neighbors without getting to know them. And we can't get to know them without careful listening. To be quick to listen means being ready to hear another person out--to hear what's on their hearts as well as on their minds. Those who are quick to listen are patient, loving listeners who take people seriously and connect with them at the heart level. They take the time and make the effort to get to know the people around them. This kind of listening undergirds all positive human relationships and is a basic element in God's second great commandment: "Love your neighbor as you love yourself" (Matt. 19:19).

Good listening calls for an attitude of humility that reflects Jesus' loving, caring heart. Paul points to Jesus as the prime example of humility, noting that he "made himself nothing" and took on the "nature of a servant." He challenges us to have "the same love" and to "look to the interest of others" (Phil. 2:2, 4, 7). Having a Jesus-kind of love in our conversations will mean giving up our desire to be heard and paying full attention to the other person. That is God's way of building loving, caring relationships.

The goal of listening is more than simply hearing and comprehending. The goal is a meaningful, feeling-level interchange that allows us to appreciate the whole person--mind, heart, and spirit--and to find common ground. Listening becomes a way to discover where God is at work in another person's life.

Fruitful conversation on spiritual issues can be opened up by non-threatening questions that invite people to report their thoughts on spiritual things. Randy Newman, in *Questioning Evangelism*, suggests five good starter questions:
- "Do you ever think about spiritual things?"
- "At what point are you in your spiritual journey?"
- "Along the way, what part, if any, has God played in your life?"
- "How do you feel about your standing before God?"
- "Do you ever wonder about life after death?"

Starter questions like these often lead to follow-up questions that demonstrate you are really hearing what the other person has said, and that you really care about what is important to them. This was the kind of conversation Jesus had with the Samaritan women. It began with a simple question: "Will you give me a drink?" but continued with a series of follow-up questions that led to the core issues of her life and the reality of who he really was (John 4:7-26).

Good questions will often lead to a give-and-take conversation in which people will ask you similar questions--or better yet, ask you for "the reason for the hope that you have." When that happens, says Peter, "be prepared to give an answer to everyone who asks you to give the reason for the hope that you have" (1 Pet. 3:15).

DISCOVER YOUR BIBLE

Proverbs 18:13
To answer before listening—that is folly and shame.

John 4:7, 9-10, 13-14 [See John 4:7-42 for the full story]
When a Samaritan woman came to draw water, Jesus said to her, "Will you give me a drink?"

The Samaritan woman said to him, "You are a Jew and I am a Samaritan woman. How can you ask me for a drink?"

Jesus answered her, "If you knew the gift of God and who it is that asks you for a drink, you would have asked him and he would have given you living water."

"Everyone who drinks this water will be thirsty again, but whoever drinks the water I give them will never thirst. Indeed, the water I give them will become in them a spring of water welling up to eternal life."

James 1:19
My dear brothers and sisters, take note of this: Everyone should be quick to listen, slow to speak and slow to become angry,

1 Peter 3:15
But in your hearts revere Christ as Lord. Always be prepared to give an answer to everyone who asks you to give the reason for the hope that you have. But do this with gentleness and respect.

SHARE QUESTIONS

1. When Jesus asked the Samaritan women for a drink, do you think it was primarily about his thirst? What seems to be his motive? What can we learn from Jesus' example?

2. What negative trait is kicking in when we are quick to speak and slow to listen? How can we guard against this tendency?

3. What happens in a conversation when a person speaks before listening? How might good listening encourage a witnessing opportunity?

4. What might cause a person to "ask you to give the reason for the hope that you have"? Why is it important to be ready to give an answer?

5. What is a good way to answer a person who asks about the reason for our hope?

GROUP SHARE TIME (20-30 minutes)
Think of a good conversational exchange you had recently. What did you like about it? Think of a disconcerting conversation. What was not good about it? Share your thoughts on these questions with each other.

Share personal joys and concerns in preparation for your group prayer time.

GROUP PRAYER TIME (10-15 minutes)
Pray with and for each other. Ask that God will give you the listening skills required to build good relationships with friends and neighbors, especially those with whom you hope to share the good news.

LIVE IT OUT (between meetings)
- Continue to remember each other in your prayers. Ask God to give you and your teammates the ability to be quick to listen.
- Pray the Word that you have studied together. *Thank* Jesus for being quick to listen to you, and *ask* for his help in listening and answering.
- Live out the Word by *being quick to listen, and by being prepared to give an answer to anyone who asks the reason for the hope you have.* Think through past experiences in which you succeeded or failed in this.

LOOK AHEAD (before the next meeting)
- Read and mark noteworthy passages in the opening commentary of Session 21.
- Discover the Bible's thoughts on *lost people matter to God.*
- Add to your *Loving People to Jesus* list if possible, and share the names of additions at your next meeting.

PART FOUR: Share (Sessions 21-29)

For weeks now you have been releasing God's power and grace into the lives of friends and acquaintances through prayer. You've also been channeling his love to them by caring. It's time now to think about how they will hear the good news that can turn their lives around and bring them home to the Father.

In this *share* section, you will be reminded of how much lost people matter to God, and how much he wants them found. You will be encouraged to think about how you can introduce them to your best friend, Jesus. You will pray for and watch for the right time to share the best news ever announced. You will think through the ABCs of receiving Christ and be prepared to share the gospel with friends, acquaintances, or loved ones who need to hear this good news.

If you are like me and many other Christians, you will probably find this section a bit daunting. Please don't let it scare you. Sharing the gospel is not as difficult and scary as we may think. It's not so difficult because God is the one who will open people's minds to the gospel and give your words power. Your prayers for the lost have prepared the way. God, who dearly loves them, has been at work in their hearts and lives in response to your prayers. Not only that, but the good news that you share with them is in itself "the power of God for salvation" (Rom. 1:16). It does what you or I could never do. Finally, as you prepare to share the gospel, remember that you are not challenging your friends to some new and difficult task. You are simply offering them a gift--the greatest and best gift the world has ever known. All they have to do is say "I accept!"

SESSION 21
Lost People Matter to God

Have you ever been lost? I got lost once in an airport in Ukraine. The connecting flight for which I was scheduled didn't exist. What must I do now? Nobody spoke English. All the signs were in Russian. I was stuck; it was panic time! I asked God to send someone to the rescue—and he did! My "savior" turned out to be a Ukrainian-born couple from New York. Phew! Thank you, Lord! I was "saved." Several hours and $600 later I was on my way again.

If you have ever been lost, you know it's a frightening experience. And when the "savior" shows up, that is a moment of great relief.

There are an awful lot of lost people in the world today, people who fumble around the airport of life unable to reach their intended destination. Hundreds of them live within a few miles of you. You probably rub shoulders with some of them—family members, friends, neighbors, coworkers—every day. They may not be panicked about their situation, but the truth is, they are in peril and they don't know how great the peril is. What's worse, they don't even know where they are going.

Lost people matter greatly to God. More than a lost sheep to a shepherd willing to leave ninety-nine sheep to search for the one. More than a lost coin to a woman scouring her house for it. Lost people matter more to God than a lost son matters to a father who watches day and night for that son to come home (Luke 15:3-24). Finding the lost is urgent business to God, who values them above anything else in all creation.

Lost people also mattered to Jesus, the Good Shepherd. Matthew reports that Jesus, seeing the crowds, "had compassion on them, because they were harassed and helpless, like sheep without a shepherd" (Matthew 9:36).

Those who don't know the Shepherd are lost. They are lonely, endangered, helpless and frightened. They need to be found. And when even just one lost sheep is found, the Shepherd's joy is so great that angels and saints join in the celebration.

Jesus has a shepherd's heart. He wants lost sheep found and brought into the fold. In fact, that is the reason that he came to earth, and the reason that he went to the cross. He said, "I am the good Shepherd; I know my sheep and my sheep know me . . . and I lay down my life for the sheep" (John 10:14-15). Of those not yet in the fold he said, "I must bring them also" (John 10:16). After finding a lost sheep named Zacchaeus, Jesus said, "the Son of Man came to seek and to save the lost" (Luke 19:10).

How does the Good Shepherd continue his work today? He does so through us. He sends us back to the pasturelands to find those sheep not yet in the fold. We go with the conviction that he will accomplish his work through us, even as he said: "I must bring them also, they too will listen to my voice, and there shall be one flock and one shepherd" (John 10:16). As under-shepherds, we value people as he valued them, have a compassion like his compassion, and eagerly tell them about the Good Shepherd, who laid down his life for the sheep.

Prayer: "We pray, Good Shepherd, that you will give us something of your passion for lost sheep. Help us to be aware of those you love who are lost and unable to find their way to you. Use us for your purposes in their lives."

DISCOVER YOUR BIBLE

Matthew 9:36
When [Jesus] saw the crowds, he had compassion on them, because they were harassed and helpless, like sheep without a shepherd.

Luke 15:3-7
Then Jesus told them this parable: "Suppose one of you has a hundred sheep and loses one of them. Doesn't he leave the ninety-nine in the open country and go after the lost sheep until he finds it? And when he finds it, he joyfully puts it on his shoulders and goes home. Then he calls his friends and neighbors together and says, 'Rejoice with me; I have found my lost sheep.' I tell you that in the same way there will be more rejoicing in heaven over one sinner who repents than over ninety-nine righteous persons who do not need to repent."

Luke 19:9-10
And Jesus said to [Zacchaeus], "Today salvation has come to this house, since he also is a son of Abraham. For the Son of Man came to seek and to save the lost." [For the whole story read Luke 19:1-10.]

John 10:10-11, 14-16
"I have come that they may have life, and have it to the full. I am the good shepherd. The good shepherd lays down his life for the sheep."

"I am the good shepherd; I know my sheep and my sheep know me—just as the Father knows me and I know the Father—and I lay down my life for the sheep. I have other sheep that are not of this sheep pen. I must bring them also. They too will listen to my voice, and there shall be one flock and one shepherd."

REFLECTION (15-20 minutes)

1. How is the condition of a spiritually lost person like that of a lost sheep? What might "harassed and helpless" look like in today's world?

2. How much do lost sheep matter to Jesus? How does your concern for lost sheep compare to that of Jesus?

3. What does the Shepherd do for lost sheep? What does Jesus expect us to do?

4. Jesus invited himself to Zacchaeus's house to save him. How does Jesus seek the unsaved now that he has returned to the Father?

5. What makes finding the lost so urgent? Who do you know that needs the full life that the Shepherd offers? What kind of scene do you imagine will take place in heaven when this person is found?

GROUP SHARE TIME (20-30 minutes)

If Jesus mingled with the lost people you rub shoulders with every day, what do you think he would feel? What would he say? Who would he send to find the lost sheep? How would he react if they were found? Share your thoughts on these questions as a group.

Share joys and concerns in preparation for your group prayer time.

GROUP PRAYER TIME (10-15 minutes)

Pray for each other's personal requests, including the following prayers:
- *Thankfulness* for the privilege of being in the fold of the Good Shepherd.
- *Confession* for failures to witness for Christ when you had the opportunity.
- *Petition* that Jesus would cause you to know his deep love for lost sheep.
- *Intercession* for those you know that are not in the fold.

LIVE IT OUT (between meetings)

- Pray for yourself and your friends, asking that Jesus will give you an awareness of the lost condition of people you know and a heartfelt concern for their spiritual well-being.
- Pray the Word by stepping into Jesus' "sandals" as you pray the Scriptures studied earlier in this session.
- Live out the Word this week *by seeing "lost sheep" as Jesus sees them, by feeling toward them what Jesus feels, and by imagining the joy of the Good Shepherd and his heavenly friends over the finding of your lost friends.*

LOOK AHEAD (before the next meeting)
- Thoughtfully read the opening comments of Session 22.
- Discover the Bible's thoughts on *your life, his story.*
- Check out *Preparing Your Personal Testimony* from Appendix C. Use it to help prepare for your contribution to the GROUP SHARE TIME at the next session.

PERSONAL NOTES

SESSION 22
Your Life, His Story

Everyone has a story to tell. If you asked me for life stories I could tell you about a harrowing fishing trip, a devastating winter storm, or a near-fatal mountain climbing experience. If you wondered about God's work in my life, I could tell you how a Bible verse changed my life, how God dealt with my pride, or about the day I trusted God and was delivered from fear of death.

You also have stories to tell. Telling stories is an important way to witness. Most of our stories are also God's stories—stories of his working in our lives and in our world. When you tell your God-stories to those who almost never think about God, you are subtly giving them evidence of God's existence. He suddenly becomes more real to them. They are challenged to think about God in new and different ways. They decide something about God based on what they have heard you say. He becomes a real person—someone to whom they can relate, someone who cares, someone who loves, maybe even someone who saves. They may not believe in the God you're describing, and they may question the reality of what you are saying, but they can't argue with what you have presented. It's *your* story.

Almost everyone knows about Psalm 23. Why is it so widely familiar and so greatly loved? Probably because it's a story. Psalm 23 tells the story of a heavenly Shepherd who cares for us, his sheep—a Shepherd who guides and provides, who comforts and protects. It's a profound message that comes to us simply, clearly, and in story form.

Another story with a profound message is the that of the Samaritan women who meets Jesus at the village well. Their conversation leads to the point where he offers her the living water of eternal life. She drinks of it and is dramatically changed. Unable to keep the good news to herself, she hurries back to her village, blurts out her story, and convinces her fellow villagers that Jesus is the long-awaited Messiah. Convinced by her story, the villagers seek out Jesus, urge him to stay, and end up becoming his followers. Her story was really Jesus story, and the story of revival in a Samaritan village. That's the power of story.

The Bible is full of stories: the story of creation, the fall, the life and death of Christ, the outpouring of the Spirit, the spread of the church. These are God stories, and they continue as he works in the lives of Christians every day. Your life story is a part of God's story, and it's worth telling. As you tell others what Christ has done and is doing in your life, you are telling Christ's story. Your story, like that of the Samaritan women, has the power to convince others about Christ and the difference he makes in people's lives.

Pray that God will give you opportunities to tell his story by telling your story. Keep in mind the following guidelines:

- Ask permission before you tell personal spiritual-experience stories.
- Use personal language and speak of emotional realities that preserve the drama of a real-life experience with a living Christ. You are telling someone about a person, not presenting a doctrine.
- Make sure your story gives credit to God and is more about him than about you.
- Use plain language. Avoid religious terms that may be unfamiliar to your hearers.
- Be honest and humble, even about your failures.
- Don't imply that others should have an experience like yours.
- Don't use the story to preach, to exhort, or to pepper people with Bible verses.
- For faith-sharing testimonies, include a life-before and life-after meeting Christ.
- Finally, keep your story short, in good taste, and to the point.

DISCOVER YOUR BIBLE

Psalm 23:1-4

The LORD is my shepherd, I lack nothing. He makes me lie down in green pastures, he leads me beside quiet waters, he refreshes my soul. He guides me along the right paths for his name's sake. Even though I walk through the darkest valley, I will fear no evil, for you are with me; your rod and your staff, they comfort me.

John 4:28-30, 39-42 (Read John 4:1-30 for the whole story.)

Then, leaving her water jar, the [Samaritan] woman went back to the town and said to the people, "Come, see a man who told me everything I ever did. Could this be the Messiah?" They came out of the town and made their way toward him.

Many of the Samaritans from that town believed in him because of the woman's testimony, "He told me everything I ever did." So when the Samaritans came to him, they urged him to stay with them, and he stayed two days. And because of his words many more became believers.

They said to the woman, "We no longer believe just because of what you said; now we have heard for ourselves, and we know that this man really is the Savior of the world."

Acts 4:20

"As for us, we cannot help speaking about what we have seen and heard."

1 Peter 3:15

But in your hearts revere Christ as Lord. Always be prepared to give an answer to everyone who asks you to give the reason for the hope that you have. But do this with gentleness and respect....

REFLECTION (15-20 minutes)

1. Psalm 23 is David's life story told in the language of shepherding. What is David telling us about his life? About his God?

2. What motivated the Samaritan woman to tell her story? How would you rate the content and clarity of her story?

3. What was the initial reaction to the Samaritan woman's story? What was the lasting effect of her witness? How can someone seek Jesus today?

4. What motivated Peter and John to speak out for Christ? What does it take for a person to get to that level of motivation in witnessing?

5. Why can a story make such a big difference? What is there about your story that could cause people to seek Jesus?

GROUP SHARE TIME (20-30 minutes)

Share personal stories with your group on one of more of the following questions. Be ready to share these and similar stories with non-Christians you know or meet.
- How did you come to faith in Christ? Was it a sudden conversion or a gradual process? What moved you forward on your faith journey?
- Do you remember a time when you failed to love God with all your heart, when you personally ignored God, when you did things you knew were wrong, or when you treated others unlovingly?
- Is there a particular Bible verse that changed your life?
- What is one of the best things about being a Christian?

Share blessings and prayer requests in preparation for the group prayer time.

GROUP PRAYER TIME (10-15 minutes)

Remember each other's prayer requests before the Lord and give thanks with and for each other.
Pray for those on your *Loving People to Jesus* list. Ask God to help you take an interest in them, to really love them, and to find ways to build relationships with them.

LIVE IT OUT (between meetings)
- Continue to pray for each other daily. Pray for opportunities to build relationships with non-Christians and to share the good news with them.
- Pray the Word used earlier in this session. Take special note of the way that Jesus cared about and related to the Samaritan woman.
- Live out the Word by preparing your personal testimony--the story of how Christ made a difference in your life.

LOOK AHEAD (before the next meeting)
- Thoughtfully read the opening comments of Session 23.
- Discover the Bible's thoughts on *what a friend is Jesus*.
- Think through the contribution you will make in the GROUP SHARE TIME at the next session.

PERSONAL NOTES

SESSION 23
What a Friend Is Jesus!

What if you had a good friend who was world-famous, a person like Abraham Lincoln or Mother Teresa? Wouldn't you be eager to introduce your other friends if you had the chance? Of course! You wouldn't want your friends to miss the opportunity to meet such a famous person. And you would be pleased to let them know that this person was truly *your* friend.

Well, you do have a world-famous friend. He is known and loved by millions of people in almost every country. His name is more widely recognized than any person in history. The book that traces his life and presents his message has been on the top of the best-seller list for centuries. His name is *Jesus.* The book of his life is the Bible. He not only lived on earth thousands of years ago; he is also alive in the world today, and you know him personally. No one ever loved you more. No one ever did more for you. He is your best friend.

Have some of your friends heard of Jesus but never personally met him? They don't think about him; they don't talk to him. They don't know that he offers eternal life as a free gift. They have no idea that he loves them and would dearly like to have a personal relationship with them. They have ignored this friend of yours, and they don't even know that ignoring him is the greatest sin of all—a sin that unless confessed and pardoned by God will lead to eternal separation from God.

Think of what it would mean for your friends to meet and come to know your best friend. And even more, think of what it would mean to Jesus, whose heart's desire it is to see your unbelieving friends come into a personal relationship with him.

Here are some things to think about if you have the opportunity to introduce your friends to Christ. First, remember that they most likely don't know many important things about Jesus. They don't know that being a Christian is about having a person-to-person relationship with Christ. They have only a vague idea of why Jesus died on the cross, why he rose from the dead. They don't know what eternal life is, and they don't think much about what comes after life on earth. They don't know that they can have a personal relationship with him. So as you introduce them to Jesus, speak plainly and carefully about these things, using words and concepts they can understand.

Second, remember that for them to meet a person whom they cannot see, hear, touch, or contact on *Facebook* will be a strange new experience for them. They may not even know that it is possible to have a real relationship with an invisible divine person. Bridge this gap by telling them about your personal relationship with Jesus. That will be more believable than anything else. Acknowledge that you have friendly conversations with Jesus every day. Tell them what it means for you to trust him, love him and serve him. Explain that eternal life is a wonderful here-and-now life as well as everlasting. Acknowledge that Jesus is truly *your* best friend, and then assure them that he wants to be *their* best friend too.

Third, remind them that Jesus is alive in the world today and is eager to help them begin a relationship with him. In fact, he is knocking at the door of their lives; he wants them to invite him into their hearts and lives. Encourage them to invite him in, to *ask* his forgiveness for ignoring him for so long, to *accept* the forgiveness that he offers, and to *commit* their lives to him. Assure them that Jesus always forgives those who are truly sorry for offending him, and always befriends those who want a relationship with him. Encourage them to talk to Jesus every day and to learn more about him from the Bible.

Pray with them and for them as often as possible in the days ahead as they grow in their friendship with Jesus. Assure them that you will continue to pray for them and will share with them in their new friendship.

DISCOVER YOUR BIBLE

Matthew 11:28-29
"Come to me, all you who are weary and burdened, and I will give you rest. Take my yoke upon you and learn from me, for I am gentle and humble in heart, and you will find rest for your souls."

John 10:9-10
"I am the gate; whoever enters through me will be saved. They will come in and go out, and find pasture. The thief comes only to steal and kill and destroy; I have come that they may have life, and have it to the full."

John 14:4-6
"You know the way to the place where I am going."

Thomas said to him, "Lord, we don't know where you are going, so how can we know the way?"

Jesus answered, "I am the way and the truth and the life. No one comes to the Father except through me."

Revelation 3:20
"Here I am! I stand at the door and knock. If anyone hears my voice and opens the door, I will come in and eat with that person, and they with me."

REFLECTION (15-20 minutes)

1. What do good friends do that makes friendship so valuable? What do we gain by friendship with Jesus?

2. What does Jesus offer to the weary? To the thirsty? To the lonely? To those whose lives are empty?

3. How would you explain to a non-Christian what it means that Jesus is "the way and the truth and the life"?

4. What important things do your unsaved friends need to know about Christ that they probably do not know?

5. What would you say if a person asked you, "How can I become a friend of Jesus?"

GROUP SHARE TIME (20-30 minutes)

Share with your group what you would say to a person who asked you to explain what it means that Jesus is your best friend. [Try to put your answer in 100 words or less, and in language that a pre-Christian would likely understand.]

Share your joys and prayer concerns in preparation for the group prayer time.

GROUP PRAYER TIME (10-15 minutes)

Cover each person in your group with heartfelt intercessory prayer. Focus prayer on not-yet-Christians using some or all of the following themes.
- *Give thanks* for all the relationships that give you the opportunity to speak of and demonstrate Christ's love to others.
- *Confess* any lack of compassion for persons you know who are on the road to an eternity separated from God.
- *Ask* Jesus to give you a heart for people like his heart.
- *Intercede* for specific persons who need to know Christ.
- *Commit* to building care/share relationships with non-Christians as God opens doors.

LIVE IT OUT (between meetings)

- Follow through on what your group prayed.
- <u>Pray the Word</u> by noting from the Scriptures studied who Jesus was, what he did and what he promised.
- <u>Live out the Word</u> *by being prepared to introduce Jesus as the one who gives rest, or as the one who gives life to the full, or as the one who is the way and the truth and the life.*

LOOK AHEAD (before the next meeting)

- Thoughtfully read the opening comments of Session 24.
- Discover the Bible's thoughts on *the best news ever.*
- Think through the contribution you will make in the GROUP SHARE TIME at the next session.

PERSONAL NOTES

SESSION 24
The Best News Ever

News is new information—usually newly released information about a recent event. Good news is news that is beneficial or favorable. What the Bible calls good news (the gospel) is the best news that has ever been announced in all of history. It is news about Jesus Christ—his life, death, resurrection and ascension to glory. It's the glad message of forgiveness and eternal life for everyone who believes.

The good news of salvation through Jesus Christ was the greatest news ever heard. It was news of the most sweeping pardon ever issued—a pardon for all past sins for those who believe. It was news of the greatest rescue ever made—the rescue of humankind from the bondage of sin and Satan. It was news of the greatest gift ever offered—the gift of eternal life. It was news that brought to light the grace, and love, and joy, and peace of God that issues into transformed life. It is news for every people group and nation in the world. It is news for all times down to this very day. No other glad announcement will ever compare to the glorious goodness of this news.

There is, of course, some bad news. The bad news is that sin separates us from God and leads to condemnation and eternal separation from God. Some people have to hear the bad news before they are ready to hear the good news. But we don't have to be afraid to share the bad news, because the bad news is trumped by the good news. The good news is that sinners who in faith seek God's forgiving grace can be pardoned for all the wrongs they have ever done and will ever do. With sin removed, once guilty sinners are reconciled to God, and welcomed into his forever-family.

The gospel is good news because it is powerful. The Bible tells us that the gospel, "is the power of God that brings salvation to everyone who believes" (Rom. 1:16). Power is the ability to influence. The power of the gospel is the power to influence what happens in the life of a person or a group of persons. The gospel is not simply a message that tells people about the power of God. It is not simply good advice that a person can take in and put to good use. It is a power from God that moves in our hearts by means of the Holy Spirit and changes our lives. It is a message that accomplishes the very salvation that it reveals. "The gospel came to you not simply with words" said Paul, "but also with power, with the Holy Spirit and with deep conviction" (1 Thess. 1:5).

God wants every person in the world to get the message of his good news. He has called us to be good-news people. "Go into all the world," said Jesus, "and proclaim the gospel to the whole creation" (Mark 16:15). The disciples, trained by Jesus, did just that. They preached the good news, and many believed and were baptized. Then many of those new believers shared the good news with still others. Luke reports: "Those who had been scattered preached the word wherever they went" (Acts 8:4).

God has continued to spread the good news to the world in the same way to this very day. By the end of the first century there was approximately one believer for every 360 people. Now, about two thousand years later, there is roughly one believer for every five people in the world. And the good news is still spreading. Those tracking the progress of the gospel tell us that more than 150,000 are coming to Christ every day worldwide. That is good news of another sort!

Who do you know that hasn't heard the good news, hasn't understood it, or hasn't sensed the value of it? Wouldn't you like to be the one to help them hear it, understand it, and know what a treasure it is? It is always fun to share good news. So go ahead and have some fun! As you have the joy of sharing good news, you'll also make God's heart glad.

DISCOVER YOUR BIBLE

Mark 16:15-16
He said to them, "Go into all the world and preach the good news to all creation. Whoever believes and is baptized will be saved, but whoever does not believe will be condemned."

Acts 10:36
"You know the message God sent to the people of Israel, announcing the good news of peace through Jesus Christ, who is Lord of all."

Romans 1:16-17
For I am not ashamed of the gospel, because it is the power of God that brings salvation to everyone who believes: first to the Jew, then to the Gentile. For in the gospel the righteousness of God is revealed—a righteousness that is by faith from first to last, just as it is written: "The righteous will live by faith."

Colossians 1:6
In the same way, the gospel is bearing fruit and growing throughout the whole world—just as it has been doing among you since the day you heard it and truly understood God's grace.

2 Timothy 1:9-10
This grace was given us in Christ Jesus before the beginning of time, but it has now been revealed through the appearing of our Savior, Christ Jesus, who has destroyed death and has brought life and immortality to light through the gospel.

REFLECTION (15-20 minutes)

1. News is new information. What new information did Christ bring to light by coming to earth?

2. What, according to the above verses, is so good about this news? What did Jesus do to make it good news?

3. How would you respond to a person who says, "What's the big deal? Why is this news so important?"

4. Who do you know that needs to hear and believe the good news? What happens to people who hear and believe? What happens to those who don't?

5. What is God's plan to spread the good news? What role would you like to have in that?

GROUP SHARE TIME (20-30 minutes)

Share with your group one or more of the positive things that happened in your life as you heard and believed the good news of Jesus Christ? Add if you can a recent experience of joy that has come from knowing the good news.

Share personal joys and concerns in preparation for the group prayer time.

GROUP PRAYER TIME (10-15 minutes)

Pray with and for each other. Expand your prayer time along the following lines:
- *Thank* God for the good news from his Word.
- *Ask* God for opportunities to share the good news with those who haven't heard.
- *Pray* that people you know who haven't heard the good news will have the chance to hear it, and will discover the way.
- *Commit* to share the good news when and if God opens the door for you.

LIVE IT OUT (between meetings)

- Pray for the personal concerns of the members of your group and for faith sharing opportunities.
- Pray the Word by praying for what is on God's heart as you discover it in the Scriptures you studied in this session.
- Live out the Word by familiarizing yourself with the **Seek and Find** gospel presentations in the appendix. Be prepared to use one or more of these.

LOOK AHEAD (before the next meeting)

- Thoughtfully read the opening comments of Session 25.
- Discover the Bible's thoughts on *turning life around*.
- Think through the contribution you will make in the GROUP SHARE TIME at the next session.

PERSONAL NOTES

SESSION 25
Turning Life Around

The English language gives us three unique phrases to describe a complete turn-around. In the military, it's called "doing an about-face." On highways, it's "making a U-turn." In everyday English, it's "doing a 180." The Bible has another term for a turn-around. It's called repentance.

You cannot help people come to faith without helping them come to grips with sin and then doing a complete turn-around. In biblical terms, they need to repent. Conversion is not simply a matter of accepting a formula or saying the right words. It's more than saying "I'm sorry, please forgive me." It's even more than just believing in Jesus. Conversion requires a turn-around, a life change that involves renouncing a past way of life and adopting a new way of life in a relationship with Christ. Repentance is absolutely essential to genuine conversion.

But talking about sin and repentance is a hard sell in today's world. Mention sin, and nonbelievers may think you are judgmental, legalistic, and narrow-minded. Yet the Bible is clear about the need to repent of sin. In his very first sermon, Peter said: "Repent, then, and turn to God, so that your sins may be wiped out" (Acts 3:19).

So how do we talk about repentance in today's culture? First, we need to help unbelievers see that sin is not just doing wrong things like lying, hating, or stealing. Sin, at its heart, is offending and breaking relationship with God—the good and gracious God who has given us life, breath, and every good thing. Sin wrongs God and alienates us from him. Sin builds walls of separation from God.

Second, people need to be aware of how their sin affects God. When we reject God's ways, he takes it personally. Spiritually disconnected people generally do not think of God as a living Person whom they have offended by failing to honor, love or trust. But the truth is, they are ignoring God and rebelling against him. That is why he withdraws from them.

Those who have alienated themselves from God must come to know that separation from God has devastating consequences. Since God is the source of all blessing, separation from God robs us of his presence and all that is best in life. Sin leads to destruction and, if not forgiven, to eternal separation from God.

True repentance is a turning around—turning from a life in which there is no relationship with God, to a relationship of love. It's a turning that involves hatred of sin on the one hand, and love for God on the other. It begins in a godly sorrow for sin that asks God to forgive; it ends in a new, life-giving relationship with God. Forgiveness is a gift from God to anyone who is truly repentant and comes seeking his forgiving grace. It's a gift available to any and all because of the life-giving sacrifice of Jesus Christ.

The reception that such a person gets with God is truly wonderful. It opens the way for full forgiveness and a new way of life, a life of love, and joy and peace in the Lord. Jesus frames the wonder of God's willingness to restore lost relationship in the story of the prodigal son, who returns home saying, "'Father, I've sinned against God, I've sinned before you; I don't deserve to be called your son again.' But the father, instead of berating the boy for his wrong-doing, calls to the servants, 'Quick. Bring a clean set of clothes and dress. Put the family ring on his finger and sandals on his feet. Then get a grain-fed heifer and roast it. We're going to feast! We're going to have a wonderful time! My son is here—given up for dead and now alive! Given up for lost and now found!' And they began to have a wonderful time.'" (Luke 15:21-24, *The Message*). To every repentant person God says: "I will remember your sin no more." The dam that has held back the river of God's delight is removed. Grace flows freely.

So should you talk to an unconverted person about repentance? Absolutely! Why? Because it is the beginning of a whole new way of life—life as a friend of God, eternal life.

DISCOVER YOUR BIBLE

Proverbs 28:13
Whoever conceals their sins does not prosper, but the one who confesses and renounces them finds mercy.

Isaiah 55:7
Let the wicked forsake their ways and the unrighteous their thoughts. Let them turn to the LORD, and he will have mercy on them, and to our God, for he will freely pardon.

Acts 3:19
Repent, then, and turn to God, so that your sins may be wiped out, that times of refreshing may come from the Lord.

2 Corinthians 7:10
Godly sorrow brings repentance that leads to salvation and leaves no regret, but worldly sorrow brings death.

1 John 1:9
If we confess our sins, he is faithful and just and will forgive us our sins and purify us from all unrighteousness.

REFLECTION (15-20 minutes)

1. What four words in these verses tell us how to deal with sin? What can prompt repentance?

2. Can you find eight positive consequences for those who do turn from sin? How will the promises in these Scripture passages change a person's life?

3. What happens to people's relationship with God when they turn from sin? What are the consequences for those who do not turn?

4. What is the status of a person who wants God's forgiveness, but doesn't turn away from sin?

5. Do you think that the spiritually disconnected people you know are aware of their alienation from God? How can you best help them?

GROUP SHARE TIME (20-30 minutes)

Share with your group any memories you have of turning around in your relationship with God. Some of these may have happened after conversion, such as turning
- from guilt to full forgiveness;
- from not knowing God to having a relationship with him;
- from ignoring God to being attentive to him;
- from self-centeredness to God-centeredness;
- from choosing your own way to following God's way.

Share prayer concerns and reasons for thanksgiving.

GROUP PRAYER TIME (10-15 minutes)

Pray with and for each other. Thank God for critical turn-arounds in your lives, especially for the one called conversion. Pray for those you know who need to make a major first-time turn-around. Offer to God your willingness to help others through this life-giving process.

LIVE IT OUT (between meetings)
- Continue to support your group friends in prayer.
- Pray the Word by focusing on turn-arounds (repentance)—any that you need to make and that you know others need to make.
- Live out the Word by *confessing any known sins, by forsaking any wrong thoughts, and by claiming times of refreshment that come from the Lord.*
- Prepare a personal testimony by reflecting on a time when you ignored God and needed to turn around and begin focusing on him.

LOOK AHEAD (before the next meeting)
- Thoughtfully read the opening comments of Session 26.
- Discover the Bible's thoughts on *the key is believing.*
- Review the gospel presentations in Appendix D to prepare for the GROUP SHARE TIME in the next session.

PERSONAL NOTES

SESSION 26
The Key Is Believing

On a warm summer day in 1955, President Dwight Eisenhower invited Billy Graham for a visit to his Gettysburg farm. After a game of golf, they settled down near a fireplace for a chat. What Eisenhower asked of Billy Graham in the moments that followed was not a prayer request nor advice on political issues. His question was, *"How can a man know for sure that he's ready to meet God . . . that he's going to heaven when he dies?"*

To answer his question, Graham opened the New Testament and shared the gospel with the president. He told him that, according to the Bible, Jesus was the Son of God, that he died for the sins of humankind, and that he was resurrected to new life. He then told him that "all who believe and accept Jesus Christ as Savior were promised forgiveness and everlasting life." Not long after that President Dwight Eisenhower was baptized—the first and only president to be baptized while in office. The key to Eisenhower's salvation was believing.

To believe means that we believe God really exists and that his Son Jesus Christ is a real person who lived on earth, died on the cross to pay the penalty for our sin, was raised to life to give us new life, and is living today in a love relationship every person who believes in him. Those who truly believe are fully forgiven and are assured of eternal life.

Believing does not mean simply saying yes to what the Bible tells us. Believing *is* about accepting the facts, but it also means confessing sin and verbally accepting God's offer of salvation—and then stepping into a growing love relationship with the living Christ. That is the heart of the Christian faith.

Jesus Christ offers to forgive our sins and cleanse our hearts so that we can have a relationship with him. He wants and cherishes a Friend-to-friend relationship with every true believer. He is committed, out of love, to do everything possible to make his friends flourish. Our personal relationship with Jesus not only guarantees us a sure place in heaven but also provides the grace that is needed to live a life of love, joy, and peace on earth. Isn't that the kind of relationship you want for family members, friends and acquaintances who have not yet come to faith?

How then can you introduce a person to Christ? Introducing two friends you know well is quite simple. If you know a little bit about each of them you can easily help them connect. But introducing a person to Jesus Christ--a spiritual person whom they cannot see, hear, or shake hands with--is not so simple. So what do you do?

First, I suggest that you tell them about your own personal relationship with Jesus. That will confirm the reality of a human person having a real and meaningful relationship with a divine person.

Second, invite them to tell you about their spiritual views by asking questions like: "So, do you believe there is a God?" "What do you think he is like?" "Do you think of Christ as a real person? "Do you think there is life after death?" Listen carefully to their ideas without being judgmental. The more you know about their beliefs, the better you will be able to help them understand what the Bible teaches.

Third, if they are interested in knowing more, assure them that God truly loves them, that he is eager to help them believe, and that he very much wants to give them eternal life. Explain that God is always listening; if they acknowledge their sin and sincerely ask forgiveness, he will forgive and give them eternal life. Explain that God will do this because Christ died to pay the penalty for sin and rose from the dead to give them new life. Encourage them to verbally confess their sin, to prayerfully accept God's offer of salvation, and to thank Jesus for saving them. Promise to pray for them and to be available to them as they deepen and strengthen their relationship with Jesus Christ.

DISCOVER YOUR BIBLE

John 1:12
Yet to all who did receive him, to those who believed in his name, he gave the right to become children of God.

John 3:16
"For God so loved the world that he gave his one and only Son, that whoever believes in him shall not perish but have eternal life."

Acts 10:43
"All the prophets testify about him that everyone who believes in him receives forgiveness of sins through his name."

Romans 5:1
Therefore, since we have been justified through faith [belief], we have peace with God through our Lord Jesus Christ.

Romans 10:9
If you declare with your mouth, "Jesus is Lord," and believe in your heart that God raised him from the dead, you will be saved.

Hebrews 11:6
And without faith it is impossible to please God, because anyone who comes to him must believe that he exists and that he rewards those who earnestly seek him.

REFLECTION (15-20 minutes)

1. What do these verses teach us to believe about God the Father? About the Father's relationship to Jesus? About God's concern for people?

2. These Bible verses ask those who want to be saved to "receive," "believe," "earnestly seek," and to say, "Jesus is Lord." How are these concepts similar? How are they different? What might they mean to a seeker?

3. Compare and contrast the ways that salvation is described in the above verses: "become a child of God," "have eternal life," "be forgiven," "have peace with God," "be justified," and "be saved." Which of these concepts would an unbeliever most likely understand? Which would be most appealing?

4. Which of these descriptions would you be most comfortable using to explain the way of salvation to a nonbeliever?

GROUP SHARE TIME (20-30 minutes)

Share with your group, in 100 words or less, how you would explain the gospel to an inquiring unbeliever.

Share what your group members need to know to pray meaningfully for you.

GROUP PRAYER TIME (10-15 minutes)

Pray for each other's needs and concerns. Pray that God will enable the members of your group to make the gospel clear to people who do not understand. In your prayer time consider
- *thanking* God for the wonder of salvation, including your own.
- *confessing* times that you have backed away from sharing the good news.
- *asking* for opportunities to lead nonbelievers to faith in Christ.
- *interceding* for those you know who are living outside the faith.

LIVE IT OUT (between meetings)
- Continue to pray for group members and for those you know who are outside the faith.
- Pray the Word, letting the Scriptures you have studied in this session inform your personal prayers.
- Live out the Word by learning the **3:16 Promise** [see Appendix D] so well that you will be comfortable using it whenever you have the opportunity.

LOOK AHEAD (before the next meeting)
- Thoughtfully read the opening comments of Session 27.
- Discover the Bible's thoughts on *the Word does the work.*
- Think through the contribution you will make in the GROUP SHARE TIME at the next session.

PERSONAL NOTES

SESSION 27
The Word Does the Work

I keep my own yard. That includes mowing lawn, tending plants, raising vegetables, and trimming several large trees. It's a lot of work, but I enjoy it--at least some of it. The one thing that makes it doable and enjoyable is having the right tools—mower, trimmer, clippers, saws, rakes, shovels, and more. Each tool is suited for a specific purpose. Some of them are even powered. There is no way I could keep my yard without these tools. They make all the difference.

When it comes to evangelism, tools also make the difference—one tool in particular, the Word of God. The Word is perfectly suited for sharing the good news. It even brings its own built-in power. There is no way we could be effective in evangelism without the Word of God. In other words, the Word does the work.

The Word provides the *message*. People must come to know who God is and what he has done for our salvation before they can believe. They need to know about Christ, his atoning sacrifice, and his life-giving resurrection. They cannot come to faith without this knowledge. Paul highlights this by asking, "How can they believe in the one of whom they have not heard?" (Rom. 10:14). John underlines the value of the Word by saying: "But these are written that you may believe that Jesus is the Messiah, the Son of God, and that believing you may have life in his name" (John 20:31).

The Word also provides the *power*. Paul calls the Word "the power of God that brings salvation to everyone who believes" (Rom. 1:16). This is not to say that the words of Scripture have some sort of magical efficacy. The power of the Word is simply the power of God. It is the Holy Spirit using the Word as a sword. It is Jesus Christ, the living Word, revealing the Father through his words and works. Through the power of the living and active Word, God's message is heard and his purposes are accomplished. Without this power, evangelism would be impossible.

The Word is *spreadable*. When Peter proclaimed the word of God on Pentecost, about three thousand believed and were baptized. Luke reports the ongoing growth of the early church: "The word of God spread. The number of disciples in Jerusalem increased rapidly, and a large number of priests became obedient to the faith" (Acts 6:7). The Word spread to Antioch, three hundred miles to the north; then, with Paul and Barnabas on mission, "the word of God continued to spread and flourish" (Acts 12:24). A few years and a few thousand miles later, the Word reached Ephesus. Luke reports, "The word of the Lord spread widely and grew in power" (Acts 19:20). God knows what he is doing. He has a powerful way to achieve his purposes.

There will, of course, be obstacles. A growing number of non-Christians do not respect the Bible as God's Word and will not respond to its use in a witnessing situation. Many post-moderns know so little about the Christian faith that they will not grasp concepts presented in biblical language. But the Word still can and does work as we tactfully engage nonbelievers in conversations about spiritual life and carefully convey fundamental truths of Scripture.

In order to work, the Word must somehow get out. It won't work if the Bible is lying on a shelf. It won't work if it is bottled up inside you. So the question is, "How are my friends going to hear the Word? How is it going to do its work in their hearts and lives?"

Here are a few suggestions. First, ask permission to bring the Bible into your conversation. Then, with their consent, share Bible thoughts or verses that speak most clearly to the issues that have surfaced. Explain thoughts and words that may be unclear to them. Invite their response by asking, "Does that make sense?" Finally, watch for future opportunities to open the Bible and take them deeper into its truths.

When it comes to evangelism, the Bible is our most useful tool. Know it well. Carry it in your heart, in your head and if possible in your hand. Give it opportunity to work.

DISCOVER YOUR BIBLE

Isaiah 55:11
"So is my word that goes out from my mouth: It will not return to me empty, but will accomplish what I desire and achieve the purpose for which I sent it."

John 20:31
But these are written that you may believe that Jesus is the Messiah, the Son of God, and that by believing you may have life in his name.

Acts 6:7 [see also Acts 12:24, 19:20]
So the word of God spread. The number of disciples in Jerusalem increased rapidly, and a large number of priests became obedient to the faith.

Romans 1:16
For I am not ashamed of the gospel, because it is the power of God that brings salvation to everyone who believes: first to the Jew, then to the Gentile.

Romans 10:17
Consequently, faith comes from hearing the message, and the message is heard through the word about Christ.

Hebrews 4:12
For the word of God is alive and active. Sharper than any double-edged sword, it penetrates even to dividing soul and spirit, joints and marrow; it judges the thoughts and attitudes of the heart.

REFLECTION (15-20 minutes)

1. What happens in the life of a person in whom the Word is working? Who is doing the work to make these things happen?

2. What do hearers have to do with the Word for it to work in their hearts? How does hearing the Word of God produce faith?

3. Share some ways in which the Word of God has worked or is currently working in your life.

4. If the "alive and active" Word is working, what is left for us to do? What may keep the Word from doing the work God intends it to do?

5. How can the Word help us be effective in evangelism? What biblical thoughts or verses might help you explain the good news to a seeker?

GROUP SHARE TIME (20-30 minutes)

How did the Word come to work in your life? Was it through a person, your family, a Sunday School class' vacation Bible School, a youth group, church services, a Bible study group, college campus meetings, a book, an evangelistic crusade?

Prepare for the prayer time by sharing personal needs, concerns, and praises.

GROUP PRAYER TIME (10-15 minutes)

Cover each other's needs, concerns and praises in a group prayer time. Consider in your prayer time:
- Your *gratitude* for the good news that God has revealed to you.
- Your *concern* for those you know who do not yet understand.
- Your *commitment* to witness to the truth found in the Word, as God opens doors of opportunity.

LIVE IT OUT (between meetings)

- Continue in daily prayer for your teammates. Ask God to use you to spread the Word.
- Pray the Word by reflecting back to God some thoughts that you gained from the Bible passages you have just studied.
- Live out the Word by trying to discern times, places, ways and relationships in which you could help to make the Word work. Offer to be God's instrument in some of these situations.

LOOK AHEAD (before the next meeting)

- Thoughtfully read the opening comments of Session 28.
- Discover the Bible's thoughts on *steps to receive Christ.*
- Think through the contribution you will make in the GROUP SHARE TIME at the next session.

PERSONAL NOTES

SESSION 28
Steps to Receive Christ

You can help your nonbelieving friends know about God and his way of salvation in their heads, but they will not be saved if he is not in their hearts. They do need to *know* about God and his way of salvation, but even more they need to *receive* Christ into their hearts.

Here are three core ideas that will draw them to Christ. First, they need to know and understand that *God loves them*, that he cares deeply about them and wants the very best for them. He wants them to have a good and beautiful life and to be full of love, joy and peace. He wants to adopt them as his children and make them members of his family.

Second, they need to know that *they can't save themselves*. Sin has driven a wedge between them and God. They have ignored him and dishonored him. As a result, they are living life apart from him. No amount of human effort can mend that broken relationship. That's bad news; but the good news is that God has provided a way for them to be made right with him.

Third, *God offers them salvation as a free gift*, a gift that they can either accept or reject. They cannot just drift into God's salvation plan. They have to opt in or they will be left out. God gives them the freedom and the help needed to make that choice. Those who make the decision and accept God's free gift receive the good, beautiful, joy-filled life that the Bible calls "eternal life." Jesus said, "God so loved the world that he gave his one and only Son, that whoever believes in him shall not perish but have eternal life" (John 3:16). Eternal life begins at the moment that the gift of new life is received and continues forever.

ABCs to Receive Christ

One simple way to help those who want to receive God's gift and have eternal life is to help them understand the ABCs of receiving Christ (A-admit, B-believe, C-commit) and to pray an ABC prayer.

First, help them to **admit** to God that they have sinned against him, and then to express their sorrow and ask forgiveness. The primary focus is admitting and repenting of living a self-centered life while ignoring God--the One who has given them life, breath, and every good thing; the One who has asked them to love him above all.

Second, help them **believe** the Bible's message that God, who is both loving and just, has done everything needed to rescue them from the punishment they deserve. Help them understand that God the Father loved the world so much that he sent his Son, Jesus Christ, into the world so that whoever believes in him would not perish but would have eternal life. Help them grasp the fact that Jesus' death on the cross was his way of paying their sin debt, and that his resurrection assures them a new and glorious life. Help them accept as true God's promise that "to all who *receive* him, to those who *believe* in his name, he gave the right to become children of God . . . children born of God" (John 1:12-13).

Third, help them **commit** to love God with all their heart, mind, and strength; and to promise they will serve him to the best of their ability. Assure them that they will be given the ability to keep this commitment by the grace of Jesus Christ and the power of the Holy Spirit, who dwells in them.

Review the following ABC prayer with those who express interest. If they are ready to receive Christ, invite them to pray these words to God from their heart. They can say the prayer by putting it in their own words, by reading the words aloud, by repeating it after you, or by means of a private prayer on their own. (Permission to copy this prayer is granted.)

> *"Dear Father in heaven . . .*
> *I **admit** that I have sinned against you by ignoring you, by not loving you with all my heart, and by not serving you. Please forgive me!*
> *I **believe** that Jesus died on the cross to forgive my sins and rose from death to give me new life. I accept your offer of full forgiveness, and I receive the new life Jesus gives me.*
> *I **commit** to loving and serving you to the best of my ability, for all the days of my life.*
> *THANK YOU for giving me "the right to become a child of God. Amen."*

DISCOVER YOUR BIBLE
Isaiah 55:6
Seek the LORD while he may be found; call on him while he is near.

Jeremiah 29:12-13
"Then you will call on me and come and pray to me, and I will listen to you. [13] You will seek me and find me when you seek me with all your heart."

John 1:12
Yet to all who did receive him, to those who believed in his name, he gave the right to become children of God.

Acts 2:37-39
When the people heard this, they were cut to the heart and said to Peter and the other apostles, "Brothers, what shall we do?"

Peter replied, "Repent and be baptized, every one of you, in the name of Jesus Christ for the forgiveness of your sins. And you will receive the gift of the Holy Spirit. The promise is for you and your children and for all who are far off—for all whom the Lord our God will call."

Acts 17:27
"God did this so that they would seek him and perhaps reach out for him and find him, though he is not far from any one of us."

Romans 10:9
If you declare with your mouth, "Jesus is Lord," and believe in your heart that God raised him from the dead, you will be saved.

REFLECTION (15-20 minutes)

1. Try to identify ten different words or phrases that describe what someone has to do in order to come to Christ.

2. What six words or phrases tell us what God promises to do for or give to those who come to him?

3. Who are the recipients of these promises?

4. Where, according to these verses, *is* God when people are trying to find him?

5. What are some things that you could do or say to help a person who wanted to enter into a relationship with Jesus Christ?

GROUP SHARE TIME (20-30 minutes)

Share with your group an experience you may have had talking with non-Christians about Christ. How did they react? Did objections surface? What was the outcome?

Each person shares personal reasons for thanks and prayer requests.

GROUP PRAYER TIME (10-15 minutes)

Thank God for each other and remember the requests that have been shared. Ask God to give you opportunities to share the gospel and to lead people to Christ.

LIVE IT OUT (between meetings)
- Regularly remember each of your group members in prayer.
- Pray the Words of Scripture that you studied in this session. Share with God your reactions to what you learned from these verses.
- Live out the Word by continuing to pray for the spiritual well-being of non-Christians in your spheres of influence. Ask God to give you the opportunity to share the good news.
- Try to get a good grasp of the ABCs of receiving Christ so that you will be able to make use them if God gives you the opportunity [Or choose one of the other gospel presentations in Appendix D].

LOOK AHEAD (before the next meeting)
- Thoughtfully read the opening comments of Session 29.
- Discover the Bible's thoughts on *eternal life is a gift*.
- Think through the contribution you will make in the GROUP SHARE TIME at the next session. At least two of the gospel presentations in Appendix D give definitions for eternal life in the **Word Meanings** section.

PERSONAL NOTES

SESSION 29
Eternal Life Is a Gift

It's not surprising that the winner of a Publishers Clearing House cash prize jumps up and down with glee. Who wouldn't? In fact, as we watch those TV ads, it's hard to resist imagining what life would be like if we were to win a lottery prize of $10,000 a week for the rest of our life.

Well, the gift I am writing about is even bigger and better than a Publishers Clearing House prize. It is something to be *really* excited about. I call it *the gift of gifts*. There is no greater, grander gift than the gift of eternal life. If you are a believer, you have already received this gift. Let me ask you to think about helping someone in your circle of acquaintances to receive this incredible gift.

First, let's understand what eternal life is. The word "eternal" makes it sound like the heart of the gift is that it is forever. Well, it is forever. But the best part is not the length. It's the quality. Eternal life is the gift of the life of Christ in us (Col. 1:27). Jesus called it "abundant life" (John 10:10). Some versions translate that as "a full and meaningful life." It's life as good as it can be, a life of perfect blessedness. Eternal life is blessed because it is life in a love relationship with the Father, through the grace Jesus Christ, and by the fellowship of the Holy Spirit. All the qualities of life possessed by God are ours when we receive this life.

And, just to be clear, eternal life does not start at some future time; it's a present possession. Once we believe in Christ we *have* eternal life. It flows into the streams of our lives here on earth. Of course, we still struggle with sin and still face challenges. But we handle these with the strength and desires of this new life. By the power of the Spirit we are able to live the abundant life.

The best thing about this wonderful new life is that it's not something we have to earn. If we had to earn it we couldn't. But we don't have to. Eternal life is a gift from God to all who come to Christ in repentance and faith. The only way to get it is from Jesus, who promised to his followers, "I give them eternal life, and they will never perish; no one will snatch them from my hand" (John 10:28). Paul also understood eternal life to be a gift: "For the wages of sin is death, but the gift of God is eternal life in Christ Jesus our Lord" (Rom. 6:23).

Paul's words remind us that the opposite of eternal life is eternal death. Death in this case means not simply the end of our bodily existence but also the absence of the abundant life that God offers in Christ. Death--life apart from

God, now and for all eternity--is the fate of those who do not believe in Jesus Christ.

Amazingly, out of his great love, God wants everyone to have this gift. Jesus made that clear in perhaps the best-known verse of the Bible: "God so loved the world that he gave his one and only Son, that whoever believes in him should not perish but have eternal life" (John 3:16).

You know people who do not have this incredible gift. You know what they're missing—and they don't! You also know the "wages" they are drawing now and will draw for eternity if they don't trust Christ. Take time to let the reality of their situation move you deeply, asking God to show you what he feels for them. Weep for those you know who are receiving the wages of sin. Let the strength of your feelings move you to earnest prayer that God will make it possible for you or someone else to share the good news of Jesus Christ with them, so that they may have this incredible gift of God.

DISCOVER YOUR BIBLE

John 5:24
"Very truly I tell you, whoever hears my word and believes him who sent me has eternal life and will not be judged but has crossed over from death to life."

John 6:40
"For my Father's will is that everyone who looks to the Son and believes in him shall have eternal life, and I will raise them up at the last day."

John 17:3
"Now this is eternal life: that they know you, the only true God, and Jesus Christ, whom you have sent."

Romans 6:23
For the wages of sin is death, but the gift of God is eternal life in Christ Jesus our Lord.

1 John 5:11-12
And this is the testimony: God has given us eternal life, and this life is in his Son. Whoever has the Son has life; whoever does not have the Son of God does not have life.

REFLECTION (15-20 minutes)

1. What is there to eternal life besides the fact that it is everlasting? Why is eternal life so incredibly valuable?

2. Several phrases in the above verses answer the question "How can a person have eternal life?" How would you answer a person who asked you that? Would you need to explain some of the words you use?

3. Eternal life is a free gift. Why have so many people not received this enormously valuable gift of God?

4. Who among your family or friends might not be sure of eternal life? How does that make you feel?

5. How can we make sure that as many people as possible have eternal life?

GROUP SHARE TIME (20-30 minutes)

Share with each other how you would respond to a person who, in the course of a conversation, asks questions like:
- What really is eternal life?
- How can I have eternal life?
- How can I be sure that I have eternal life?

Tell the others in your group how they can pray for you.

GROUP PRAYER TIME (10-15 minutes)

Give thanks for your fellow group members and intercede in their behalf.

In your prayer time consider also:
- Praying for those you know who do not have eternal life.
- Praying that your church may be effective in reaching out to those who are not yet part of the family of God.
- Praying for those who have recently come to faith and who need to grow spiritually.
- Pray also for God to guide your group in the next phase of your journey—discipling new converts or immature believers.

LIVE IT OUT (between meetings)
- Pray by name for each one of your fellow group members.
- Pray the Word from this session *thanking* God for the amazing promises they contain and *asking* for many to hear and believe these promises that come from the heart of God.
- Live out the Word. Watch for God-given opportunities to share the five affirmation verses in the addendum with persons who do not possess eternal life.

LOOK AHEAD (before the next meeting)
- Thoughtfully read the opening comments of Session 30.
- Discover the Bible's thoughts on *discipling new Christians.*
- Think through the contribution you will make in the GROUP SHARE TIME at the next session. Check out the **Next Steps** material of Appendix E which addresses the issue of spiritual growth.

PERSONAL NOTES

PART FIVE: Aftercare (Sessions 30-37)

Having worked your way through the sections on praying, caring, and sharing, you are now ready to think about *aftercare*. The assumption is that if those you've been praying for have come to Christ, they will need your help to grow spiritually. Or you may know some young or immature believers who need to grow in grace and knowledge. Whatever the case, this section focuses on their need to grow in the faith. Just as infants need mature adults to care for them and help them grow, so do new believers.

Jesus commanded his own disciples to disciple others, teaching them to obey everything he commanded (Matt. 28:20). Discipling immature Christians or new believers means teaching them how to pray, helping them learn to read and meditate on the Word of God, and walking hand in hand as they learn to live the Christian life.

Young believers also need to be connected with others in the body of Christ and enfolded into the Christian community. The writer of Hebrews challenges believers to "spur on one another to love and good deeds" and to meet together regularly (Heb. 10:25). Three of the *aftercare* sessions will focus on enfolding new believers into the church.

The early church apparently understood the need for good aftercare. From the book of Acts we learn that new believers in the Jerusalem church "devoted themselves to the apostles' teaching and the fellowship, to the breaking of bread and to prayer" (Acts 2:42). That's a good model to keep in mind as you help young Christians grow strong in the Lord.

SESSION 30
Discipling New Christians

Babies are born virtually helpless. They can't walk; they can't talk; they can't feed themselves. They need lots of help in order to make it to adulthood. It's much the same with newborn believers. They don't know what it means to "walk in the Spirit." They don't know how to feed on the Word. They still can't verbalize their faith. They need lots of help to grow up spiritually.

That's where you come in. If you are a mature believer, you are in a position to be a spiritual "parent."

Discipling is basically a matter of helping young believers grow in spiritual maturity by adhering to the words of their Lord. The young believers in your life may be small children, they may be mature adults who have recently come to faith, or they may be long-term believers whose development has been arrested. Think of how limited your faith knowledge was when you first came to Christ. That is where most new believers are in their faith journeys, no matter how old they are. Think of what they don't know yet. They need someone older in the faith and wiser in the ways of the Lord to take them by the hand. And, like newborn babies, they need this help promptly.

When Jesus commanded his followers to make disciples, he wasn't just urging us to go for more and more converts. He was also challenging us to bring new converts to the place where they are ready "to obey everything I had commanded them" (Matt. 28:20). New disciples who come up to that standard are men and women who have moved "beyond the elementary teaching about Christ" to the point of full spiritual maturity (Heb. 6:1). Christ's challenge to us is to make that happen in those who are new to the faith.

Young believers need help in many ways. They need help knowing how to study the Bible, how to pray, how to worship, how to witness, and how to use their spiritual gifts in ministry. They need to understand what it means to be born again, to be justified by faith, sanctified by the Spirit, dead to sin, and alive to Christ. Peter summarized this growth process by urging believers to "grow in the grace and knowledge of our Lord and Savior Jesus Christ" (2 Pet. 3:18). Do you know someone who needs that kind of help?

Learning to live as a Christian also means learning to live in community. New believers need to be welcomed into the church. Robert Webber observed that "the church itself is the womb of disciple-making."[1] Jerusalem's new Spirit-filled church developed depth and intimacy by "[devoting] themselves to the apostles' teaching and to fellowship, to the breaking of bread and to prayer" (Acts 2:42). New Christians also need the kind of deeper, shared-life experiences that are fostered in small groups. Jesus did his best discipling in the context of small groups of three to twelve.

The Christian way is not only taught, it is also caught. Paul not only challenged Timothy to command and teach important spiritual truths but to "set an example for the believers in speech, in conduct, in love, in faith and in purity" (1 Tim. 4:12). Jesus' teachings and illustrations were usually anchored in intimate, daily activities like fishing, making bread, herding sheep, sowing seeds, harvesting crops, and lighting lamps. What daily activities in your relationships will help you disciple those you care about?

It takes a disciple to make a disciple. If you are a disciple of Christ and you have new Christian friends, then you are in the best possible position to help them grow in Christ. Prepare yourself by thinking through what these new Christians don't yet know. Ask yourself what you can share with them to help them grow. Pray that God will give you the time and opportunity to disciple; then step into the discipling role for which God has fitted you.

1. Robert E. Webber, *Ancient-Future Evangelism*, p.74.

DISCOVER YOUR BIBLE

Matthew 28:18-20
Then Jesus came to them and said, "All authority in heaven and on earth has been given to me. Therefore go and make disciples of all nations, baptizing them in the name of the Father and of the Son and of the Holy Spirit, and teaching them to obey everything I have commanded you. And surely I am with you always, to the very end of the age."

Acts 2:42
They devoted themselves to the apostles' teaching and to fellowship, to the breaking of bread and to prayer.

Colossians 3:16
Let the message of Christ dwell among you richly as you teach and admonish one another with all wisdom through psalms, hymns, and songs from the Spirit, singing to God with gratitude in your hearts.

1 Timothy 4:11-13
Command and teach these things. Don't let anyone look down on you because you are young, but set an example for the believers in speech, in conduct, in love, in faith and in purity. Until I come, devote yourself to the public reading of Scripture, to preaching and to teaching.

2 Timothy 2:1-2
You then, my son, be strong in the grace that is in Christ Jesus. And the things you have heard me say in the presence of many witnesses entrust to reliable people who will also be qualified to teach others.

REFLECTION (15-20 minutes)

1. What does it take to make a convert? To make a disciple? What is gained as new believers get discipled?

2. What important things do disciple-makers do to make disciples? What resources can they draw on? What is your church doing to make disciples?

3. How does our lifestyle affect our ability to disciple? Is there anything about your example in speech, conduct, love, faith, and purity that you would not want a new believer to imitate?

4. Who discipled you? Who needs you to disciple them?

5. What is Christ's role in our disciple-making ministries?

GROUP SHARE TIME (20-30 minutes)

Share with each other the most important steps you have taken toward full spiritual maturity. Who or what helped you the most? What difference did this growth make in your spiritual journey?

Share blessings and prayer requests.

GROUP PRAYER TIME (10-15 minutes)

Give thanks for God's personal blessings and intercede on each other's behalf. Pray that Christ's discipling vision, recorded in Matthew 28:18-20, will become clear and compelling for your group and your spiritual community. Ask the Lord what role he has for you when it comes to discipling others.

Pray for immature believers and new converts who need to grow in grace, in knowledge, and in obedience to everything Christ commanded.

LIVE IT OUT (between meetings)
- Pray for significant spiritual growth for yourself and your friends in Christ.
- Pray the Word you have just studied.
- Live out the Word by looking for ways to help believers—young or old, recent converts or long-term Christians--to "obey everything Christ commanded."

LOOK AHEAD (before the next meeting)
- Thoughtfully read the opening comments of Session 31.
- Discover the Bible's thoughts on being *vitally linked to Christ.*
- Think through the contribution you will make in the GROUP SHARE TIME at the next session.

PERSONAL NOTES

SESSION 31
Vitally Linked to Christ

By the time Jesus went to the cross he had lived with his disciples for about three years. They must have been surprised that, after telling them that he was leaving them (John 13:33), he went on to talk about *remaining* with them. They soon came to understand, as we now know, that though he was leaving them physically, he was remaining with them in a spiritual way.

I am using the phrase "vitally linked" in the title of this introduction to lay hold of the idea, inherent in the original Greek, that our connection with Christ is a living one. To "be in" or "remain in" Christ is to be joined to him in such a way that his life is shared with us. Christ's life—a life of supreme quality and everlasting duration—goes far beyond the physical. It is derived from God and conveys the very life of God to those who are vitally linked to him. So to remain in Christ is to have an unbroken, life-giving connection with Jesus and with God the Father. Jesus' ascension to heaven was not the last step in the salvation plan. For Christ, who ascended, has now descended with the coming of his Spirit, living out his life in and through his followers on earth.

When Paul says in Galatians 2:20, "I no longer live, but Christ lives in me," he is saying that his thoughts are infused with Christ's thoughts, his emotions are touched by Christ's emotions, and his actions are the actions of Christ. When a child lives in a mother's womb, the umbilical cord attaching the child to mother transmits her oxygen, her nourishment, her very life to the child. You and I are attached to Christ by means of an invisible cord that will never be severed. Our lives have become an extension of his. Our love, joy, peace, and faith are extensions of his. Without Christ, there is no spiritual life. "Apart from me," said Jesus, "you can do nothing" (John 15:5).

New believers need to understand that it's not just the *work* of Christ *for* them that gives them life. It is also the *person* of Christ *within* them. It's not just Christ's death that makes a difference; it's also his ongoing life that transforms us. Salvation is not just getting to heaven by and by; it's a new reality in the present--Christ living in us. Those who come to faith are only at the starting line. They need to move into a growing love relationship with the living Christ.

What can you do to help new Christians live vitally linked to Christ? Here are four ideas. First, share with them your own experience of Christ living in you. Be as down-to-earth and practical as you can.

Second, use real-life comparisons to deepen their understanding. Jesus used the vine/branches metaphor recorded in John 15:1-8 to illustrate the value of having a life-receiving connection with him. Paul described Christ's vital connection to believers by comparing him to the head of a body, with his people making up the various parts of the rest of the body (1 Cor. 12:12-27). Don't be afraid to use contemporary illustrations like the umbilical cord or others you discover.

Third, read together and unpack the meaning of key passages like: John 14:20, 23; John 15:1, 4-10; Gal. 2:20; and 2 Pet. 1:3-4, which speak of our union with Christ.

Fourth, encourage new believers to read through the accounts of Jesus' life in the gospels, trying to see their lives in the narratives of his life, and the narratives of his life in their own real-life experiences.

The living link they have with Christ is not just life *from* him. It is Christ himself--a thinking, feeling, willing, talking, listening, active Person--living in them. In other words, he who once lived in his own physical body on earth is alive on earth today in each one of his followers.

No one ever lived a more loving, joyful life on earth than Jesus. Now we, who live in him as he lives in us, are privileged to share in his loving, joyful, good and beautiful life in the days of *our* lives here on earth. Wow! What a privilege.

DISCOVER YOUR BIBLE

John 15:1, 4-8
"I am the true vine . . . Remain in me, as I also remain in you. No branch can bear fruit by itself; it must remain in the vine. Neither can you bear fruit unless you remain in me.

"I am the vine; you are the branches. If you remain in me and I in you, you will bear much fruit; apart from me you can do nothing. If you do not remain in me, you are like a branch that is thrown away and withers; such branches are picked up, thrown into the fire and burned. If you remain in me and my words remain in you, ask whatever you wish, and it will be done for you. This is to my Father's glory, that you bear much fruit, showing yourselves to be my disciples."

2 Corinthians 5:17
Therefore, if anyone is in Christ, he is a new creation. The old has passed away; behold, the new has come (ESV).

Galatians 2:20
I have been crucified with Christ and I no longer live, but Christ lives in me. The life I now live in the body, I live by faith in the Son of God, who loved me and gave himself for me.

1 John 3:24
The one who keeps God's commands lives in him, and he in them. And this is how we know that he lives in us: We know it by the Spirit he gave us.

REFLECTION (15-20 minutes)

1. John 15:1-10 describes a real-life, person-to-person relationship. Read the verse out loud. substituting the phrase "stay vitally linked to[1]" in place of the phrases "remain in," "live in" and "in" wherever it fits in the verses above. What insights does that give you?

2. Why is having a vital link with Christ so important for believers? What are the results of such a linkage? How will this link affect our prayer lives?

3. What does fruit in a Christian's life look like? What "old" has passed away, what "new" has come if a person is linked to Christ (2 Cor. 5:17)?

4. What, according to these verses, is the Son's role in our lives? The Father's role? The Holy Spirit's?

5. Why might the idea of being "in Christ" be difficult for a new believer to comprehend? Can you think of a modern-day metaphor that would shed light on this idea (e.g., electric power, wi-fi, etc.)?

[1] <u>Vitally</u> means "in a manner that imparts life"

GROUP SHARE TIME (20-30 minutes)

List and share with each other as many blessings as you can think of that would be missing in your life if you were not vitally linked to Christ.

Share your personal prayer requests. Take this time also to share with each other areas of life in which you would like to make spiritual gains in the days ahead.

GROUP PRAYER TIME (10-15 minutes)

Pray for each other's personal requests and as well as for desired spiritual gains.

Give thanks for the spiritual blessings in your lives that come from a living relationship with Jesus Christ.

LIVE IT OUT (between meetings)

- Cover your fellow group members in prayer. Give thanks for spiritual blessings and continue to pray for spiritual riches yet to be gained.
- Pray the Word you have studied in this session. Ask the Holy Spirit to help you stay vitally linked to Christ. Ask God to enable you to help other believers to abide in Christ.
- Live out the Word by remaining vitally linked to Christ. Notice the fruit that is already in your life. Watch for new fruit.

LOOK AHEAD (before the next meeting)

- Thoughtfully read the opening comments of Session 32.
- Discover the Bible's thoughts on *experiencing God through prayer*.
- Think through the contribution you will make in the GROUP SHARE TIME at the next session.

PERSONAL NOTES

SESSION 32
Experiencing God Through Prayer

Do you remember the first word you ever said—perhaps "dada" or "mama"? Though you may not remember, it was an important moment in your life. No doubt your parents were excited to hear that first word. They probably repeated it back to you and then you began echoing it back to them. Before long you were talking in short sentences. Still, it took years before your communication skills were fully developed.

It was also momentous when your new Christian friends first began talking with God--they confessed their sin, asked God's forgiveness and promised to serve him. Now they will have to develop their ability to converse with God, to grow in an ongoing experience of God in prayer. That, once again, is where you come in.

How can you help them? The first thing is to pray *for* them. It's important for them to pray regularly, but they will face hindrances. The apostle Peter encouraged his readers to "be clear minded and self-controlled so that you can pray" (1 Pet. 4:7). The devil, aware of their new faith commitment, will do everything possible to discourage prayer. What's more, they aren't used to carving out time for prayer. That's something they will have to learn. Encourage them to set aside a daily quiet time with God. Your prayers for them will make a difference, as God enables them by his Spirit to pray.

Also watch for opportunities to pray *with* them. Just as you learned to talk by hearing others talk, they will learn to pray by hearing you pray. Conversing with real feeling to someone who is alive but unseen will be new to them. Let them hear you pray from your heart and not just your head. It must be clear to them that you are conversing with a real Person--your all wise, every-where-present loving Father, with whom you have a very real relationship. Let them sense how easy, natural, and enjoyable it is to pray.

Help your new Christian friends understand that prayer is essentially a love relationship. It's the conversational part of the most important love relationship in their lives. Understood as a love relationship, *praise* becomes a way for them to express their love and admiration for God. *Thanksgiving* is a way to express gratitude for God's gifts of love.

Confession is a way to acknowledge sorrow for sin's offenses and find forgiveness. *Petition* is a way to claim the promises of the Father, who out of love offers them his richest and best gifts. *Intercession* is a way to partner with him by releasing his power and grace into people's lives. *Submission* is a way of saying, "God, I love you and I choose to serve you." Prayer is all about enjoying and living in a true, deep, meaningful love relationship God.

When Jesus' disciples asked him, "Lord, teach us to pray," he gave them a model that we know as the Lord's Prayer. It is not a magic formula to be mechanically repeated. Rather, it's a summary of the fundamental truths that should be on our hearts when we pray. The opening words, "Our Father in Heaven" remind us of the intimacy of our relationship with God. The first three petitions invite us to pray for God's greatest concerns--his glory, his kingdom, and his will. They remind us that God should have first place in our lives. The next three petitions focus on our greatest human needs: our physical needs ("give us our daily bread"); our need for pardon ("forgive our debts"); and our need for spiritual protection ("deliver us from the evil one"). They remind us that we can't live the Christian life without the Father's grace and protection. Jesus, who taught this prayer to his disciples, would surely be disappointed if new generations of believers were not taught it too. That's where you come in.

Helping new Christians experience God through prayer is both a great privilege and a huge responsibility. Do it well and you will be handing your friends in Christ a key to the best love relationship they will ever know.

DISCOVER YOUR BIBLE

2 Chronicles 7:14
"If my people, who are called by my name, will humble themselves and pray and seek my face and turn from their wicked ways, then I will hear from heaven, and I will forgive their sin."

Jeremiah 29:11-13
"For I know the plans I have for you," declares the LORD, "plans to prosper you and not to harm you, plans to give you hope and a future. Then you will call on me and come and pray to me, and I will listen to you. You will seek me and find me when you seek me with all your heart."

Matthew 6:7, 9-13
"And when you pray, do not keep on babbling like pagans, for they think they will be heard because of their many words.

"This, then, is how you should pray: 'Our Father in heaven, hallowed be your name, your kingdom come, your will be done, on earth as it is in heaven. Give us today our daily bread. And forgive us our debts, as we also have forgiven our debtors. And lead us not into temptation, but deliver us from the evil one.'"

Mark 1:35
Very early in the morning, while it was still dark, Jesus got up, left the house and went off to a solitary place, where he prayed.

Luke 5:16
But Jesus often withdrew to lonely places and prayed.

SHARE QUESTIONS

1. Who is able to pray with the assurance that God will hear? What promises does God make to those who meet his prayer requirements?

2. What plans does God have that should encourage us to pray? How might praying the Lord's Prayer make those plans a reality?

3. There are eight plural pronouns (we, us, our) in the Lord's Prayer. What do these plural pronouns teach us about prayer? (Matt. 6:7, 9-13)

4. What would you conclude about Jesus' prayer life, based on Matt. 6:9-13, Mark 1:35 and Luke 5:16?

5. What is the difference between pagan prayer and Christian prayer? What will it take to help new believers have a heart-to-heart connection with God when they pray?

GROUP SHARE TIME (20-30 minutes)

Share with your group how you experience God through prayer. What is your reaction to the thought that prayer is the most important love relationship in your life? To what extent is that a reality? What qualities of Jesus' prayer life would you most like to emulate in your own?

Report to each other those areas where God has answered prayer and those areas where you have need of prayer.

GROUP PRAYER TIME (10-15 minutes)

Lift each other up in prayer, giving thanks for the blessings of a love relationship with God through prayer.

Remember especially those areas in your prayer lives that need more attention.

Pray for immature believers you know who need help to grow in prayer.

LIVE IT OUT (between meetings)

- Bless your teammates by praying for them.
- Pray the Word that you have studied this week. Practice applying the God-first perspective of the first three petitions of the Lord's Prayer into your other prayers.
- Live out the Word by continuing to pray for more and better prayer in your own life, in the lives of new believers you know, and in your faith community. Be alert to God-given opportunities to mentor new believers in prayer.

LOOK AHEAD (before the next meeting)

- Thoughtfully read the opening comments of Session 33.
- Discover the Bible's thoughts on *living by the Word.*
- Be ready to share your spiritual growth experience at the beginning of next week's session.

PERSONAL NOTES

SESSION 33
Living by the Word

Many things we do in life have a pay-off. People who faithfully invest in retirement accounts tend to have well-funded retirements. People who exercise regularly tend to have stronger bodies and better health. The pay-off principle also works in the spiritual realm. Christians who regularly meditate on the Word of God have well-nourished spiritual lives, like trees planted by streams of water. Those who live by the Word, says the Psalmist, are going to be wise, refreshed, joyful, and enlightened (Psalm 19:7-8).

Scripture is wonderfully clear on the blessings enjoyed by those who live in accord with God's will. I am particularly impressed with God's word to Joshua: "Meditate on [this book of the law] day and night, so that you may be careful to do everything written in it. Then you will be prosperous and successful" (Josh. 1:8). Prosperity and success sounds like the American dream; but we know better. God is not promising Joshua financial wealth or material prosperity. He is promising him, and all those who live by the Word, spiritual prosperity and success.

Probably no passage of Scripture sends a clearer message about the worth of God's Word than Paul's words to Timothy: "All Scripture is God-breathed and is useful for teaching, rebuking, correcting and training in righteousness, so that the servant of God may be thoroughly equipped for every good work" (2 Tim. 3:16-17). Scripture's value stems from the fact that it comes from God. It's God-breathed. Though written by human beings out of their own experiences and in their own writing style, it is God's Word because God guided the authors to write what he wanted them to write. People who study Scripture and learn from it are guided, corrected, safeguarded, and equipped for service in the kingdom.

And it is not only the written Word that accomplishes that. The ever-present author is with us through his Spirit to work the truths of his Word into our hearts and lives. He is there to teach, convict and train person-to-person. He is there to equip us for the good work he would have us do for his glory and his kingdom.

All this being true, it is critically important to help new believers learn to live by the Word. By helping them to study and know the Scriptures we are helping them be spiritually prosperous and successful, to be trained in righteousness, and to "stay on the path of purity" (Ps. 119:9). We are helping them weather storms by building their lives on the solid foundation of Jesus and his words (Matt. 7:26-27).

If I had a good architectural blueprint and tried to build a house based on the drawings, I am sure I'd fail miserably. But if I had a knowledgeable building contractor working by my side and overseeing my work, I think that I could do it. You and I are like building contractors working side by side with novices who are constructing their spiritual houses. It's an extremely important role. Let's do it carefully and prayerfully. Let's help them meditate regularly on the Word and "do everything written in it," so they will know the spiritual prosperity and success that God has promised.

DISCOVER YOUR BIBLE

Joshua 1:8
"Keep this Book of the Law always on your lips; meditate on it day and night, so that you may be careful to do everything written in it. Then you will be prosperous and successful."

Psalm 19:7-8
The law of the LORD is perfect, refreshing the soul. The statutes of the LORD are trustworthy, making wise the simple. The precepts of the LORD are right, giving joy to the heart. The commands of the LORD are radiant, giving light to the eyes.

Psalm 119:9-11
How can a young person stay on the path of purity? By living according to your word. . . . I have hidden your word in my heart that I might not sin against you.

Matthew 7:26-27
"Everyone who hears these words of mine and puts them into practice is like a wise man who built his house on the rock. The rain came down, the streams rose, and the winds blew and beat against that house; yet it did not fall, because it had its foundation on the rock. But everyone who hears these words of mine and does not put them into practice is like a foolish man who built his house on sand. The rain came down, the streams rose, and the winds blew and beat against that house, and it fell with a great crash."

2 Timothy 3:16-17
All Scripture is God-breathed and is useful for teaching, rebuking, correcting and training in righteousness, so that the servant of God may be thoroughly equipped for every good work.

REFLECTION (15-20 minutes)

1. What will life be like for those who put the Word of God into practice? What is there about the Word that makes a quality Christian life possible?

2. What must a person *do* with the Word in order to have a rich spiritual life?

3. What counter-strategy do you think the devil and his minions are hatching in the darkness of the netherworld?

4. What storm-related destruction have you seen in the lives of people around you? What guiding principles, from the Word of God, could have helped them avoid those crashes?

5. Who helped you to live by the Word? Who do you know that needs your help to live by the Word?

GROUP SHARE TIME (20-30 minutes)

What elements in your group experience of the past months--Bible study, life sharing, prayer with and for each other, accountability--have contributed the most to your spiritual growth? What do you think new or under-developed Christians could learn from what you have experienced?

Share your most urgent prayer requests as well as your reasons for gratitude.

GROUP PRAYER TIME (10-15 minutes)

Continue to cover each other in prayer. Give thanks for the spiritual gains that you have made in the last several months, and reference some of the specific means that God used.

Fold some thoughts from the Scriptures you have just studied into your group prayer time.

Pray for spiritual growth opportunities for new or spiritually undeveloped Christians you know.

LIVE IT OUT (between meetings)

- Support your fellow group members in your ongoing prayers.
- Pray the Words that spoke to you in Session Thirty-Three. *Thank* God for the spiritual gains he has given you through the Word. *Ask* God to make you more and more a person of the Word.
- Live out the Word by asking God to show you how you can help under-developed believers grow in grace and knowledge. Encourage family members, friends and/or new Christians to adopt good Bible study habits.

LOOK AHEAD (before the next meeting)

- Thoughtfully read the opening comments of Session 34.
- Discover the Bible's thoughts on *devoted to one another*.
- Think through the contribution you will make in the GROUP SHARE TIME at the next session.

PERSONAL NOTES

SESSION 34
Devoted to One Another

In the natural world, animals and birds often travel or hunt in groups—so commonly, in fact, that we have collective names for them. Fish swim together in a school, an army of ants trek together, lions form a pride, dolphins frolic in a pod, butterflies swarm to make up a flutter, and a group of floating otters makes a raft. Words like *pack*, *herd*, *flock*, and *colony* are used to describe groups of many different species. Such creatures form groups out of both need and desire. They look out for each other, but they also seem to enjoy each other's company.

Believers also come together to form groups called churches, congregations, or families of God. In these groups, we look out for each other and enjoy each other's company. Christian living is a matter of belonging with others in the same family. God's community provides love, support and accountability. These values are foundational to the spiritual health, growth, and protection of its members.

The love that binds believers together is first of all the love of Christ. Without it, there would be no Christian community, no loving devotion of the type that binds us together. Christ's love flows to us--and through us to others--in the family of God.

The new believers of the first church in Jerusalem—a church planted by Jesus' disciple—formed the kind of community that he had in mind. Luke tells us, "They were together and had everything in common . . . they continued meeting together . . . they ate together . . . praising God and enjoying the favor of all the people" (Acts 2:42-47). Paul urges the believers in Rome to "be devoted to one another in love" (Rom. 12:10). The apostle John challenges believers to "love one another" (1 John. 4:7). Peter longs for readers to "have sincere love for each other. . . from the heart" (1 Peter. 1:22). Scripture could hardly be more clear. Love--the kind of love that gives unsparingly for the well-being of others--was a critical element in the life of the New Testament church.

The first Christians did not have church buildings or billboards. They didn't have church bulletins or Bibles to carry to the meetings. They didn't have Sunday School curriculums or hymnals. They had never been to a church growth conference, and yet they turned the world upside down. How did they do it? Critical to their success was the fact that they created authentic community--the community of Christ. It was a community that attracted people, a community in which people's needs were met, a community that gave clear evidence of their faith. They created a community of love, a love so obvious and authentic that observers knew these believers were born of God and knew God (1 John 4:7).

If you have followed through on the fundamental concepts of this *Loving People to Jesus* course, you are probably involved in the lives of some who have made new commitments. You may also know some one-time believers who have fallen away from the faith or have become estranged from Christian community. Begin praying for them. Ask God to draw them to himself and to the place he has for them in the community of Christ. Ask God to give them spiritual friends who will walk with them and help them find a place in Christian community. Tell God that you are willing to be one of those friends if he wants you to. Include them in your circle of friends in as many ways as possible. Devote yourself to them in love.

DISCOVER YOUR BIBLE

Acts 2:44-47
All the believers were together and had everything in common. They sold property and possessions to give to anyone who had need. Every day they continued to meet together in the temple courts. They broke bread in their homes and ate together with glad and sincere hearts, praising God and enjoying the favor of all the people. And the Lord added to their number daily those who were being saved.

Romans 12:10, 13, 15-16
Be devoted to one another in love. Honor one another above yourselves. . . Share with the Lord's people who are in need. Practice hospitality. . . Rejoice with those who rejoice; mourn with those who mourn. Live in harmony with one another.

Hebrews 13:1-2
Keep on loving one another as brothers and sisters. Do not forget to show hospitality to strangers, for by so doing some people have shown hospitality to angels without knowing it.

1 Peter 1:22
Now that you have purified yourselves by obeying the truth so that you have sincere love for each other, love one another deeply, from the heart.

1 John 4:7
Dear friends, let us love one another, for love comes from God. Everyone who loves has been born of God and knows God.

REFLECTION (15-20 minutes)

1. What did the early Christians do that made their community so attractive?

2. How would you describe the quality of life in a Christian community that lives up to God's standards? How does your church compare?

3. What light do the above verse shed on God's role in authentic Christian community? How do they help us understand Christian love?

4. What factors in today's culture make it difficult to create communities of love? What can churches do to build such communities?

5. What practical things could you do to help spiritual seekers or new believers experience Christ-like love?

GROUP SHARE TIME (20-30 minutes)

Share with each other what it has meant to you to be part of this support group in which you were devoted to each another. Share also, if you can, one or more ways that you have been blessed by being part of a broader Christian community.

Share prayer requests and the need(s) of family members or friends.

GROUP PRAYER TIME (10-15 minutes)

Give thanks for the blessings you have received from each and from your church. Cover each other's prayer requests by praying around the circle or doing popcorn prayers.

Pray for persons who may not have experienced love and blessing in Christian community. Pray also for others you know who need that kind of love right now.

LIVE IT OUT (between meetings)

- Cover the other group members in prayer, and give thanks for the blessings that you have received from your group as well as from the broader Christian community.
- Pray the Word by meditating on the Scripture passages that you have just studied and responding to the divine Author of these words.
- Live out the Word by *loving each other deeply, showing hospitality to strangers,* and *living in harmony with one another.*

LOOK AHEAD (before the next meeting)
- Thoughtfully read the opening comments of Session 35.
- Discover the Bible's thoughts on *finding a place to grow.*
- Think through the contribution you will make in the GROUP SHARE TIME at the next session.

PERSONAL NOTES

SESSION 35
Finding a Place to Grow

If I were a flower, the place where I would most like to grow would be in a botanical conservatory. Conservatory custodians do everything possible to create favorable growing conditions for their plants. They choose the best soil. They keep the soil well fertilized and watered. They provide the right climate by controlling the temperature and humidity levels. They make sure each plant has enough space and gets the right amount of sunlight and shade. In that kind of hothouse environment, plants flourish and grow to their fullest potential.

A loving, encouraging Christian community provides the kind of climate that will best help believers grow spiritually. In the church, or in a small group with other Christians, we can be loved, forgiven, embraced, prayed for, and mentored in the faith. There we can find warmth, friendship and acceptance. The Christian community is the best place to grow. Of course, there are unhealthy churches and uncaring groups, but that is not God's norm.

An overriding theme in the New Testament is the unique responsibility that church members have for each other. The apostle Paul urged Thessalonian Christians to "encourage one another and build each other up" (1 Thess. 5:11) and expressed his conviction that the Lord would "make [their] love increase and overflow for each other and for everyone else" (1 Thess. 3:12). He convinced the Ephesians that by "speaking the truth in love" they could "grow to become in every respect the mature body. . . of Christ" (Eph. 4:15-16). The writer of Hebrews challenged believers to "spur one another on toward love and good deeds" (Heb. 10:24).

When disciples band together and pool their abilities and resources, they have incredible potential to promote spiritual health and growth. Each member brings different gifts, abilities, and interests. Each has a different personality and relational style. Together they can accomplish what no one of them could do alone. This potential was fundamental to building the New Testament church.

The dynamic of love in Christian community also has implications for evangelism. Jesus said, "By this all men will know that you are my disciples, if you love one another" (John. 13:35). The world has the right to judge our authenticity by what they see in our relationships. Jesus' final prayer for all believers was that we might "be brought to complete unity," so the world would know that the love we share comes from the Father (John 17:23). The Father is still answering Jesus' prayer today.

Those new to the faith have a lot to learn. Most have little knowledge of the Bible, minimal experience with the church, and no sense of Christ-like behavior. They need to learn how to *read and meditate on the Word of God* if they are to be "thoroughly equipped for every good work" (2 Tim. 3:16-17). They need to learn how to *pray* "in the Spirit on all occasions with all kind of prayers and requests" (Eph. 6:18). They need to learn to *worship* in spirit and in truth (John 4:24), to do their part in the *work* of the Lord (Eph. 4:16), and to be his *witnesses* (Isa. 43:10). They need to learn to love and be loved. Without basics like these they are liable to fall back into old patterns of thinking and behavior.

New believers who are *enfolded* into a community of committed, loving believers will be strengthened and encouraged. They will be built up in the faith, will grow to become mature in Christ, and will be spurred on to love and good deeds. In other words, they will find a place to grow. When we learn to live together in humble, loving community we receive a life and peace that few others ever know. What a wonderful thing we can do for our Lord and for his new followers. Isn't that the kind of community your covenant group wants to create?

DISCOVER YOUR BIBLE

1 Thessalonians 3:2, 12-13
We sent Timothy, who is our brother and co-worker in God's service in spreading the gospel of Christ, to strengthen and encourage you in your faith. . . May the Lord make your love increase and overflow for each other and for everyone else, just as ours does for you. May he strengthen your hearts so that you will be blameless and holy in the presence of our God and Father when our Lord Jesus comes with all his holy ones.

1 Thessalonians 5:11
Therefore encourage one another and build each other up, just as in fact you are doing.

Ephesians 4:15-16
Speaking the truth in love, we will grow to become in every respect the mature body of him who is the head, that is, Christ. From him the whole body, joined and held together by every supporting ligament, grows and builds itself up in love, as each part does its work.

Hebrews 10:24-25
And let us consider how we may spur one another on toward love and good deeds, not giving up meeting together, as some are in the habit of doing, but encouraging one another—and all the more as you see the Day approaching.

REFLECTION (15-20 minutes)

1. What are believers in a Christian community urged to do for each other?

2. What will happen in a Christian community where Christ-followers do what these Scriptures propose? What will go wrong if they don't?

3. How might the evil one try to counteract God's plan to help new believers grow spiritually?

4. (Eph. 4:15-16) What is Christ's role in building Christian community? What does the head/body metaphor in these verses teach us about spiritual community?

5. Who do you know that might need to be lovingly embraced in Christian fellowship or spurred on to love and good deeds? How might you be involved in their lives?

GROUP SHARE TIME (20-30 minutes)

Share with your group some of the ways that God has "strengthened your heart" in the last few years. Who did God use to spur you on? Whom might God want you to spur on?

Share with your group some specific way that they can pray for your faith to be "strengthened and encouraged."

GROUP PRAYER TIME (10-15 minutes)

Pray for each member of your group to be strengthened and encouraged in the faith.

Pray that the Christian community you are part of may be a place where believers grow spiritually.

LIVE IT OUT (between meetings)
- Intercede for your fellow team members, being especially mindful of specific ways they need to be strengthened.
- Pray the Scriptures in this session for yourself and for others. Pray that your church will find effective ways to help believers to grow spiritually.
- Live out the Word by *encouraging and building each other up, speaking the truth in love,* and *by spurring one another on to love and good deeds.*

LOOK AHEAD (before the next meeting)
- Thoughtfully read the opening comments of Session 36.
- Discover the Bible's thoughts on *sharing life together.*
- Think through the contribution you will make in the GROUP SHARE TIME at the next session.

PERSONAL NOTES

SESSION 36
Sharing Life Together

It's wonderful to be part of a Christian community. Think for a moment what it means to you. You know the people in your fellowship and they know you. You arrive at a meeting and they look you in the eye, greet you with a smile, and shake your hand or give you a hug. They ask you about yourself, listen to your answer, and respond in an affirming way. They are glad to see you because they really care about you. You feel welcome! What you are experiencing is Christian fellowship--the mutual enjoyment of healthy love relationships.

Fellowship begins, said John, as we share in the life of the Father and his Son, Jesus Christ. But then we share the life he gives to us with others as "we walk in the light" and "have fellowship with one another" (1 John 1:3,7). In other words, the bonds that link us to Christ also link us to one another. That kind of intimacy can only be found in authentic Christian community.

From the very beginning, believers in the Christian community shared life together. Acts tells us that they were "one in heart and mind." They shared their possessions and everything they had (Acts 4:32-34). Each one used his or her God-given abilities to serve others. They were a fellowship—a group of individuals with the same interests—sharing life, sharing hopes, sharing joys and sorrows. That is what God intended the church to be.

Those new to Christ have not known this kind of fellowship before coming to faith. They need to be warmly welcomed into a Christian community where they can enjoy true fellowship. Surveys confirm that unless new believers form several new faith-based friendships in the first six months of their spiritual journey, they will likely fall away from the faith. Seventy-five percent of those who have fallen away, when asked the reason, indicated that no one cared if they became part of the community of believers or not.

What should those new to faith expect to find in the family of God? They should expect to find the Christ-like love that Jesus commanded: "Love each other as I have loved you" (John 15:12). They should expect to find mutual caring and burden-bearing (Gal 6:2). They should sense God's presence in communal worship. They should sense heartfelt love for God as we pray together. Above all, they should experience God's love in a new and personal way as they are warmly welcomed and fully accepted into the shared love-life of a Christ community.

New believers should be encouraged not only to enjoy the benefits of membership in the body of Christ but also to fulfill the responsibilities. They need to *learn how to love*. Christ-like love—living for others—is not common in Western culture, but it is God's norm. Newborn believers, with the ever-loving Christ in their hearts, will have a new love for fellow believers, as well as for those who are not yet believers. You can help new believers understand the meaning of love and the human longing for authentic relationships. Help them to take an increased interest in others, to listen carefully, and to reach out sensitively. They will find this to be more exhilarating than they could have imagined.

Sharing in Christian community is vital to knowing Christ. To be effective, evangelism must first lead people to Christ and then into the shared life of Christian community. New believers will not experience the wholeness that God intends unless they can share in the fellowship of God's people. If they are not yet ready to become a member of a local church, then consider introducing them to a small group of believers who are at a similar place in their spiritual journey. It's in such a group that they will most likely find the meaningful relationships and loving acceptance that their hearts long for.

Disciples are learners. They need to learn to love God above all and their neighbor as themselves. They need to know how to give and receive love as members of the fellowship of Christ. Who better to help them than someone like you, who has already experienced the shared life of a local community of Christ.

DISCOVER YOUR BIBLE

Acts 2:42
They devoted themselves to the apostles' teaching and to fellowship, to the breaking of bread and to prayer.

Acts 4:32-34
All the believers were one in heart and mind. No one claimed that any of their possessions was their own, but they shared everything they had. . . . And God's grace was so powerfully at work in them all that there were no needy persons among them.

Ephesians 2:14, 19
For he himself is our peace, who has made the two groups one and has destroyed the barrier, the dividing wall of hostility. . . . Consequently, you are no longer foreigners and strangers, but fellow citizens with God's people and also members of his household.

1 Peter 4:8-10
Above all, love each other deeply, because love covers over a multitude of sins. Offer hospitality to one another without grumbling. Each of you should use whatever gift you have received to serve others, as faithful stewards of God's grace in its various forms.

1 John 1:7
But if we walk in the light, as he is in the light, we have fellowship with one another, and the blood of Jesus, his Son, purifies us from all sin.

REFLECTION (15-20 minutes)

1. What good things happen in a Christian community when believers share life together?

2. What makes it possible and natural for believers to share life together?

3. What gifts (unique abilities) have you received from God to serve others? (1 Peter 4:10)

4. What is the problem with trying to live the Christian life apart from Christian community? Where do non-Christians look for community?

5. Do you know someone who needs to be welcomed into a group of believers who sharing their lives? What can you do to make that happen?

GROUP SHARE TIME (20-30 minutes)

Share with your group some positive experiences you have had as part of a Christian community.

Share with each other your personal needs, concerns and ongoing reasons for thanksgiving.

GROUP PRAYER TIME (10-15 minutes)

Pray over the needs and concerns you shared earlier. Give thanks to God for the ways that he has worked in each of your lives.

Pray for the fellowship needs of new believers, especially those that you know well.

LIVE IT OUT (between meetings)
- Intercede for your fellow team members, being especially mindful of their greatest needs.
- Pray the Bible passages you have studied into the fabric of your own spiritual life.
- Live out the Word by *sharing what God has given you with others, and by using your spiritual gifts to serve others.* Pray for Christian groups that give new believers a place to grow.

LOOK AHEAD (before the next meeting)
- Thoughtfully read the opening comments of Session 37.
- Discover the Bible's thoughts on being *qualified to multiply*
- Think through the contribution you will make in the GROUP SHARE TIME at the next session.

PERSONAL NOTES

SESSION 37
Qualified to Multiply

By the time Jesus had finished training his disciples, those eleven were qualified to multiply. He prepared them to do what he had been doing, and "even greater things than these" (John 14:12-14). He told them they had been chosen and appointed to bear much fruit--"fruit that will last" (John 15:16). He even prayed for those who would "believe in [him] through their message" (John 17:20). Just before ascending he emphasized their new role as "witnesses in Jerusalem, and in all Judea and Samaria, and to the ends of the earth" (Acts 1:8).

And multiply they did. It started with Peter's first post-Pentecost message; three thousand believed and, were baptized (Acts 2:41). It continued as "the Lord added to their number daily those who were being saved" (Acts 2:47). Soon "the number grew to about five thousand" (Acts 4:4), and on beyond that "more and more men and women believed in the Lord and were added to their number" (Acts 5:14). Talk about multiplication!

Paul was also thinking of multiplication when he said to Timothy, his protégé, "the things you have heard me say in the presence of many witnesses entrust to reliable people who will also be qualified to teach others" (2 Tim. 2:2). Did you catch it? Truth communicated through five stages--first Paul, then Timothy, then reliable people, next qualified teachers, and finally the others whom they would teach.

If you are completing this *Loving People to Jesus* study, you are now hopefully qualified to multiply. You have discovered the value of accountability in a ministry team. You have built group members up by loving and praying for each other. Together you have learned how to defeat the enemy and win over sin. You have prayerfully released God's power and grace into the lives of non-believers and have worked to build caring relationships with them. You have honed faith-sharing skills and sought opportunities to witness. You are now qualified to multiply by sharing what you have gained with others who would benefit from a similar experience.

I was so excited by my first support fellowship group about forty years ago that I asked my group to release me to go out and start some new support groups. Within a few months two new groups started. In the years that followed the multiplication continued. Like Timothy, we entrusted what we had learned to others qualified to teach, and they in turn enlisted others.

How can you go about birthing new groups? First, share your testimony every chance you get with individuals, with fellowship groups, or even with a whole church. Tell them your story. Show them the material you have used and briefly explain how the *Loving People to Jesus* study works. Give them some hints on how to find group participants who have a similar interest, and some ideas on how to form a group. Answer their questions. Offer them prayer support. You might even offer to lead a couple of start-up sessions for them.

As you think and pray about multiplying your group experience, think about this. A team of five typically has an impact on at least fifteen spiritually disconnected persons. If your group birthed two more groups, and those groups each birthed two groups, those seven groups would be spreading the good news to over one hundred people. And of course, with God's blessing it can go way beyond that. Do you see the potential impact of that kind of multiplication? Maybe Jesus had something like that in mind when he said of seed that fell on good soil, "It came up, grew and produced a crop, multiplying thirty, sixty, or even a hundred times" (Mark 4:8).

DISCOVER YOUR BIBLE

John 15:16
"You did not choose me, but I chose you and appointed you so that you might go and bear fruit—fruit that will last."

Acts 1:8
"But you will receive power when the Holy Spirit comes on you; and you will be my witnesses in Jerusalem, and in all Judea and Samaria, and to the ends of the earth."

Acts 5:14; 8:4 [See also Acts 2:41, 47; 4:4; 19:12]
Nevertheless, more and more men and women believed in the Lord and were added to their number. . ... Those who had been scattered preached the Word wherever they went.

Acts 13:47-49
"For this is what the Lord has commanded us: 'I have made you a light for the Gentiles, that you may bring salvation to the ends of the earth." . . . And all who were appointed for eternal life believed. The word of the Lord spread through the whole region.

2 Timothy 2:1-2
You then, my son, be strong in the grace that is in Christ Jesus. And the things you have heard me say in the presence of many witnesses entrust to reliable people who will also be qualified to teach others.

REFLECTION (15-20 minutes)

1. What made the gospel spread so rapidly in the church? What will make this type of fruitfulness possible today?

2. Who was spreading the gospel in the early church? Who is spreading the gospel today?

3. How well is the church doing at spreading the gospel today? How can we do better?

4. What implications do Paul's instructions to Timothy in 2 Tim. 2:1-2 have for the transmission of the gospel? How can a small group facilitate this happening today?

5. What was the role of the Father, of the Son, and of the Holy Spirit in the spread of the gospel? Are they still functioning in the same way today?

GROUP SHARE TIME (20-30 minutes)

Share with your group times, places, or ways that you have seen the gospel spread. What methods of witnessing seem to work well? Share ways of witnessing that have worked for you.

Share personal prayer requests and reasons for thanks with your group.

GROUP PRAYER TIME (10-15 minutes)

Pray over the joys and concerns that group members shared. Thank God for ways in which God has used you to reach out to reachable people.

Ask God to raise up new *Loving People to Jesus* groups to reach reachables.

LIVE IT OUT
- Regularly remember each of your group members in prayer. Continue to pray for the spiritual well-being of non-Christians you know.
- Pray the Scriptures you have just studied into your life. Ask God to help you start new *Loving People to Jesus* groups.
  Live out the Word by *bearing fruit, being his witnesses,* and *spreading the word of the Lord in your community.*

LOOK AHEAD
- Who among your friends or acquaintances might be blessed by a *Loving People to Jesus* experience like yours? Decide when and where you might be able to introduce them to this course and the possibilities it has for them and their "reachable" friends.
- Consider providing a copy of the course for those you encourage to start covenant groups.
- Look for an opportunity to share your groups experience in your church or some large-group context.

PERSONAL NOTES

APPENDIX A

My *Loving People to Jesus* List

My Commitment: "I commit myself, Lord, with your help, to pray for, care for and share the gospel with the following persons as you make that possible!"

Help me, Lord:
- ➢ To faithfully <u>pray</u> with a burden that reflects your burden for those named below.
- ➢ To lovingly <u>care</u> in ways that convey your love and grace to them.
- ➢ To clearly <u>share</u> the good news so that they may believe and be saved.

- _____
- _____
- _____
- _____
- _____
- _____
- _____
- _____
- _____
- _____

APPENDIX B

Biblical Ways to Pray for Seekers

1. **Pray that God the *Father* will <u>draw them to Christ</u>.**
   John 6:44 – *"No one can come to me unless the Father who sent me draws him."*

2. **Pray that *Christ* will <u>seek and save them.</u>**
   Luke 19:10 – *"For the Son of Man came to seek and to save the lost."*

3. **Pray that the *Spirit* will <u>open their eyes</u> and turn them from darkness to light.**
   Acts 26:18 – *"Open their eyes and turn them from darkness to light, and from the power of Satan to God, so that they may receive forgiveness of sins."*

4. **Pray that they will <u>come to their senses</u> and go to the Father to confess their sin.**
   Luke 15:17-18 – *"When he came to his senses, he said. . . 'I will set out and go back to my father and say to him: Father, I have sinned against heaven and against you.'"*

5. **Pray that they will <u>believe in Jesus</u> and have eternal life.**
   John 3:16 – *"For God so love the world that he gave his one and only Son, that whoever believes in him shall not perish but have eternal life."*

6. **Pray that they will be <u>discipled to obey Christ</u> in everything.**
   Matthew 28:19-20 --*"make disciples. . . teaching them to obey everything I have commanded."*

Suggested Ways to Use These Prayer Prompts

1. Pray these prayers for specific individuals or groups of people you care about who do not know Christ.

2. Set aside a special time to pray with your ministry team or with a select group of believers for the unsaved people you know.

3. Invite family members to make a list of their acquaintances who don't know Christ, and then pray together for those named.

APPENDIX C

Prepare Your Personal Testimony

Your personal testimony is the story of how Christ made a difference in your life. It's easy for you to share because it's *your* story. It's easy for others to listen to because it's a story, and people love to hear stories. But even more than that, it's Christ's story—the story of how he changed your life. He is the really important person in your story. He made the changes you experienced. Your personal testimony is the story of how the real and living Christ changed you. It makes Christ believable and confronts your hearers with a reality that they may not have thought about before. It challenges them to think about Christ as a living person.

Telling your story can have a powerful impact, especially on an unbeliever. It demonstrates the validity of true faith and makes them wonder about having such a faith. It reveals the reality of a personal relationship with Jesus Christ and makes them think about the possibility of such a relationship. It subtly suggests that the One who has changed you could also change them. And because it is not an idea or a theory, it's not something that they can argue with. It's a true story. They simply have to deal with it.

To be a well-equipped witness for Christ, you'll want to spend some time preparing your personal testimony. The Bible reminds us to "always be prepared to give an answer to everyone who asks you to give the reason for the hope that you have. But do this with gentleness and respect" (1 Peter 3:15). Take time to write out your testimony in 100 words or less. Try to include all the basic elements of the gospel--repentance, faith, and obedience. Be sure to capture God's part in the process. Include, if possible, the following elements:

- What my life was like before I knew Jesus
- How I came to know that I needed Christ
- What happened as I trusted Christ to save me
- What difference Christ has made in my life

Take some time to practice sharing your testimony with Christian friends. Let them help you sort out the best, the clearest and most compelling elements in your story and to advise you on parts that you might be able to leave out.

Life Lessons

You might also want to prepare a few brief life-lesson stories to use with pre-Christian friends. Use the following opening lines to jog your memory and get you started:

- I grew the most in my faith when I . . .
- One way that I discovered peace of mind was . . .
- Jesus became more real to me when . . .
- One person who helped me grow spiritually was . . .

APPENDIX D

Seek and Find

SESSION 1

The 3:16 Promise

John 3:16 is the best-known verse in the Bible. In 26 words, it tells us of God's *WIDE-REACHING* love, his *AMAZING* gift, a desired and *DOABLE* human response, and the *EVERLASTING* consequences of simply saying: "Yes, God, I accept." God's *love* is more than affection. It means that he cares for us so deeply that he wants our highest good. God's *one and only Son* is Jesus Christ. That God *gave* him to the world means that he sacrificed his Son to save human beings from hell; Jesus died on the cross to pay the penalty for our sin. That we should *not die* means that we will not have to live apart from God forever. *Eternal life* is a blessed and beautiful life that begins here and now and lasts forever. To *believe* is to accept this amazing gift that God offers.

****

Bible Verse:
"*God so loved the world that he gave his one and only Son. Anyone who believes in him will not die but will have eternal life.*" --John 3:16

You may share personal thoughts or ask any question about this verse now or during our discussion.

1. What main idea leaps out at you from this verse?

2. How does this portrayal of God compare to ideas you have had about God?

3. What do we learn here about God's primary concern for people who live in his world?

4. Do you think God's gift of his one and only Son solves the problem that He is concerned about?

5. What does it mean for a person to *believe* something? What do you think it means to believe in Christ?

6. What do you think it's like to have eternal life?

Step-of-Faith Prayer

"Father, I believe that you do love the world and that you love me. I believe that you gave your one and only Son to die for my sins so I can live forever with you. I understand that apart from you I will perish. I accept your gift of forgiveness and the blessed and beautiful life that you offer me. Thank you, Lord Jesus! Thank you! Amen."

Group Share Time: Members share their **personal history**, such as where they were born, their family, schooling, employment, and so on. [5-6 minutes each.]

Word Meanings:

3:16 *God* -- "God" is not a name, but a title. The name of the first person of the Trinity is Father.

3:16 *gave* -- That God gave means that the Father sent his Son to do what had to be done to save human beings from the penalty of sin. To do this Jesus had to die on the cross and suffer the torments of hell. He came back to life (resurrection) to give us new life and returned to heaven to rule over the world. He and the Father sent the third Person of the Trinity--the Holy Spirit--to live with and in all who believe.

3:16 *One and only* -- That God has a one and only Son means that his Son has God's nature and is equal to him. His Son is truly God.

3:16 *anyone* – "Anyone" includes every person who truly believes, no matter how bad they may have been. God wants everyone to believe and be saved.

3:16 *believe* -- To believe in God means, first of all, to accept as true that God exists and that he always keeps his promises to us. Beyond that, it means that we confidently accept his offer of salvation and agree to love and serve him.

3:16 *not die* – The death referred to here is a spiritual death; it means a life apart from God. To ignore God during our days on earth is to experience a kind of death. If we remain separated from God to the end of our lives, the separation becomes permanent. That is known as hell.

3:16 *eternal life* -- Eternal life is more than a life that lasts forever. It is a wonderful, ongoing love relationship with God that leads to a truly blessed life, beginning here on earth and lasting for all eternity.

SESSION 2

ABCs to Receive Christ

To **admit** is to *confess* to God that you are truly sorry for the sins you have committed against him by living a self-centered life and ignoring him. To **believe** is to *trust* that Jesus Christ, who paid for sin by dying on the cross, will forgive you every wrong thing you have done and will cleanse your heart, if you ask him to forgive you. Those who do not ask will remain unforgiven. To **commit** is to *promise* God that you will love and serve him for the rest of your life. Everyone who *admits*, *believes*, and *commits* receives eternal life--a good and beautiful life in friendship with God, beginning now and lasting forever.

****

Bible Verses:
Admit:
But God is faithful and fair. If we confess our sins, he will forgive our sins. He will forgive every wrong thing we have done. He will make us pure. --1 John 1:9

Believe:
"Anyone who believes in the Son has eternal life. Anyone who does not believe in the Son will not have life. God's anger remains on them." --John 3:36

Say with your mouth, "Jesus is Lord." Believe in your heart that God raised him from the dead. Then you will be saved. --Romans 10:9

Commit:
"Not everyone who says to me, 'Lord, Lord,' will enter the kingdom of heaven. Only those who do what my Father in heaven wants will enter." --Matthew 7:21

Reflect Questions:

1. What do these verses teach us about God? About Jesus?

2. What do these verses teach us about the human predicament?

3. Who, according to these verses, receives eternal life? How can a person be sure of eternal life?"

4. Would you say that being saved is quite complicated or fairly simple (Romans 10:9)?

5. If people choose not to believe in the Son of God, what are they really choosing?

6. What is there about God's ABC salvation plan that makes sense to you? Are there parts that do not make sense?

Step-of-Faith Prayer

"Dear Father in heaven . . .
I admit that I have sinned against you by ignoring you, by not loving you with all my heart, and by not serving you. Please forgive me!
I believe that Jesus died on the cross to forgive my sins and rose from death to give me new life. I accept your offer of full forgiveness and the good and beautiful life that you are giving me.
I commit to love and serve you to the best of my ability, for the rest of my life. THANK YOU for giving me "the right to become a child of God. Amen."

Group Share Time:

Share with your group, if you are comfortable doing so, your thoughts on any of the following questions:
- Do you ever pray? If so, what do you experience?
- Are you quite conscious of God, or mostly unconscious of him? What are your thoughts about God?
- Does the idea of a commitment to love and serve God scare you? What might be scary about it? What could be good about it?

Word Meanings:

1 John 1:9 *forgive* -- For God to forgive means that he cancels the debt of our sin. God does not simply overlook sin. Rather, he removes our sin when we confess it and ask his forgiveness. He does so because of the sacrificial death of Jesus on the cross. God's forgiveness releases us to live truly good lives.

John 3:36 *believe* -- To believe in God means, first of all, to accept as true that God exists and that he will absolutely keep his promises to us. Beyond that, it means that we confidently accept his offer of salvation through Jesus Christ and choose to live for him.

John 3:36 *eternal life* -- Eternal life is more than a life that lasts forever. It means having an ongoing love relationship with God that results in a wonderful life here on earth and a continuing, joyous life in heaven.

John 3:36 *anger* -- God's anger (also called *wrath*) is his reaction to those who reject him and his life plan for them. Believers, having been fully forgiven, are no longer under God's anger. God holds back his anger against unbelievers to give them opportunity to repent.

Romans 10:9 *raised from the dead* -- Jesus was raised from death three days after he was crucified. His resurrection is a key element in our faith. It is the proof that he is the Son of God, that all his claims are true, and that he is alive today. It is also our guarantee that death has been forever conquered and that a richly blessed life is now our destiny.

Matthew 7:21 *kingdom of heaven* -- A kingdom is a realm over which a king reigns. The kingdom of heaven is the spiritual realm over which God reigns through his Son. Jesus Christ, our King, having defeated Satan and delivered us from his power, now rules over us and within our hearts. Christ's kingdom is a present reality in which the blessings of his reign are experienced by all believers.

SESSION 3

Coming Home to the Father

This story has been called the greatest short story in the world. It is often referred to as the story of the prodigal son, but it is more the story of a loving father. The son's offenses against his father are serious, but the amazing message here is the story of the father's loving welcome of his wayward son and the son's joyful restoration to his true home and family.

****

The Story of the Loving Father -- Luke 15:11-24

[11] Jesus continued, "There was a man who had two sons. [12] The younger son spoke to his father. He said, 'Father, give me my share of the family property.' So the father divided his property between his two sons.

[13] "Not long after that, the younger son packed up all he had. Then he left for a country far away. There he wasted his money on wild living. [14] He spent everything he had. Then the whole country ran low on food. So the son didn't have what he needed. [15] He went to work for someone who lived in that country. That person sent the son to the fields to feed the pigs. [16] The son wanted to fill his stomach with the food the pigs were eating. But no one gave him anything.

[17] "Then he began to think clearly again. He said, 'How many of my father's hired servants have more than enough food! But here I am dying from hunger! [18] I will get up and go back to my father. I will say to him, "Father, I have sinned against heaven. And I have sinned against you. [19] I am no longer fit to be called your son. Make me like one of your hired servants." ' [20] So he got up and went to his father.

"While the son was still a long way off, his father saw him. He was filled with tender love for his son. He ran to him. He threw his arms around him and kissed him.

[21] "The son said to him, 'Father, I have sinned against heaven and against you. I am no longer fit to be called your son.'

[22] "But the father said to his servants, 'Quick! Bring the best robe and put it on him. Put a ring on his finger and sandals on his feet. [23] Bring the fattest calf and kill it. Let's have a feast and celebrate. [24] This son of mine was dead. And now he is alive again. He was lost. And now he is found.' So they began to celebrate."

Reflect Questions:

1. When the son gets away from home, what does his behavior tell us about his reason for wanting to leave? What message did his leaving send to his father?

2. What does the son lose by being away from his father's home? What makes him come to his senses?

3. What is the son thinking as he is heading home (Luke 15:17-20)?

4. Describe the father's reception of his home-coming son. What makes it clear that he truly loves his son, despite his wrongdoings?

5. What does this story tell us about our heavenly Father's attitude toward spiritually wayward sons and daughters?

6. What lessons are there for us in this story?

Step-of-Faith Prayer

The prayer of a wayward son or daughter:

Dear Father in heaven, I was wrong in leaving the home and the life you provided me. I wasted what you gave me on selfish pursuits. My life has been miserable. I have sinned against you. Please forgive me and let me come back, even though I don't deserve it. I am willing to serve you, even in a lowly position.

The welcome of your loving Father:

Dear son/daughter, I am delighted that you have come back. I love you so much! I have been watching for you and waiting for this day. Let's go in and get out of these rags into a royal robe. Let's find that special gold ring you used to wear. I am so happy. Let's throw a party and celebrate this day with the whole family.

Group Share Time

Share with your group (if you feel free to do so) any memories you have of turning around in your relationship with God. This could include turnings such as
- from guilt over sin, to seeking forgiveness;
- from not knowing God, to having a relationship with him;
- from ignoring God, to being attentive to God;
- from self-centeredness, to God-centeredness;
- from choosing your own way, to following God's way.

Word Meanings:

15:12 *give me my share of the estate* -- This was a shocking request. By Jewish law the younger son would receive one-third of the inheritance after his father died. That he would ask before his father's death showed deep disrespect. It was equivalent to saying, "I wish you were dead!" The son wanted his freedom and the money but not his father.

15:13 *wasted his money*-- He lost everything and hit bottom.

15:17 *began to think clearly* -- He realized what a mistake he had made in leaving his father and decided to go back. Those who are running away from God need to come to this point.

15:20 *his father was filled with tender love* -- His watching and waiting father was ready to receive him back. Our Father watches and waits patiently for us to come back to him.

15:20 *threw his arms around him* -- The father's embrace clearly demonstrates his love. That is our Father's way of welcoming any son or daughter home.

15:21 *Father, I have sinned. . . against you* -- Worse than his wild living was what he had done to his father. Our worst sin is forsaking God, our Father.

15:22 *bring the robe. . .a ring. . .the sandals* -- The robe was a symbol of honor, the ring a sign of authority, and sandals a mark of sonship (servants went barefoot). Our Father restores returning sons and daughters to full dignity and privilege.

15:23 *Let's have a feast and celebrate* -- The Father was delighted to share his joy with his prodigal son and with the whole family. Our Father experiences great joy when we come back to him.

15:23 *This son. . .was lost. . .now he is found.* The son, once wasting his life in hopeless pursuits, had found his true home.

SESSION 4
The Roman Road

The "Romans Road" is a series of seven Bible passages from the New Testament book of Romans that clearly presents the central truths of the Christian faith. These passages make it clear that the important thing in our relationship to God is not what we can do for God, but what God has done for us. We can't earn our salvation. And we don't have to. All we need to do is accept what God offers us.

****

Bible Verses

Everyone has sinned. No one measures up to God's glory. --Romans 3:23

But here is how God has shown his love for us. While we were still sinners, Christ died for us. --Romans 5:8

When you sin, the pay you get is death. But God gives you the gift of eternal life. That's because of what Christ Jesus our Lord has done. --Romans 6:23

Say with your mouth, "Jesus is Lord." Believe in your heart that God raised him from the dead. Then you will be saved. --Romans 10:9

Everyone who calls on the name of the Lord will be saved. --Romans 10:13

Those who belong to Christ Jesus are no longer under God's judgment. --Romans 8:1

Brothers and sisters, God has shown you his mercy. So I am asking you to offer up your bodies to him while you are still alive. Your bodies are a holy sacrifice that is pleasing to God. When you offer your bodies to God, you are worshiping him in the right way. ² Don't live the way this world lives. Let your way of thinking be completely changed. Then you will be able to test what God wants for you. And you will agree that what he wants is right. His plan is good and pleasing and perfect. --Romans 12:1-2

Reflect Questions:

There is a flow in these verses that moves from the problem to the solution to the benefits, and then to a lifestyle.

1. What is the problem presented here (Romans 3:23)? Is this *really* a problem today? Is this a problem for you?

2. What moved God to do something about the problem? How did God show his love for us (Romans 5:8)?

3. What was Christ's role in solving the problem of sin (Romans 5:8, 10:9)?

4. What do we have to do to receive the benefits of God's solution? What's important about saying, "Jesus is Lord" (Romans 10:9, 13)?

5. What benefits do we get from opting in? How will this affect our lifestyle (Romans 8:1, 12:1-2)?

6. Have you opted into God's solution? What, if anything, might be keeping you from opting in?

Step-of-Faith Prayer

Dear Lord Jesus, I know that I am a sinner and that I have gone my own way. I am spiritually dead unless you save me. I believe that you died for my sin and rose from the dead. Please forgive my sin and give me eternal life. I know that you want what is best for me, so I ask you to run my life. I promise to try to live in a way that pleases you. Thank you, Jesus, for being my Savior and my Lord. Amen.

Group Share Time:

What has this group meant to you? Has your life been changed in any way by this group experience?

Word Meanings:

3:23 *God's glory* -- God's standards for our lives.

5:8 *while we were still sinners* -- Even before we turned our lives around.

5:8 *Christ died for us* -- Christ paid the penalty for our sin by his death on the cross. He was our substitute. Imagine that you are ten minutes away from being electrocuted for crimes you have committed, and the most admired person in the world steps up and says, "I love you and I am offering to die in that chair instead of you." What would you say?

6:23 *the pay you get is death* -- Pay is what we earn. "Death" in this phrase is not physical death but eternal separation from God, the source of all true life.

8:1 *no longer under God's judgment* -- No longer guilty; no longer on "death row."

10:9 *say "Jesus is Lord"* -- Acknowledge that Jesus is the supreme ruler of the world and of my personal life.

10:9 *God raised him from the dead* -- God showed that he approved of his Son's death on behalf of sinners by bringing him to life again. He gave him a new, perfect body that would never weaken or die. Jesus lives in heaven today with that body.

10:13 *calls on the name of the Lord* -- Asks the Lord to save from the penalty of sin.

12:1-2 *offer our bodies* -- Be willing to serve God in all that we do; put our energies at God's disposal.

12:1-2 *your way of thinking be completely changed* -- Having a Christlike mindset that motivates a new way of life.

SESSION 5
Meet My World-Famous Friend

I have a world-famous friend who is the best, the most powerful, and the most famous person who ever lived. He is the only person who ever lived a perfect life. He lived on earth over two thousand years ago and died on a cross. After death, he rose again to a new life. He then ascended to heaven and now rules the universe. I want you to meet him. His name is *Jesus Christ*.

He is known and loved by millions of people in almost every country of the world. His name is more widely recognized than any other person in history. The book that records his life--the Bible--has been on the top of the best-seller list for centuries.

Jesus is not only alive "up there" in heaven. He is also alive in the world today. He continues to live with and in the hearts of those who believe in him. He even calls them friends. Imagine that! Imagine being the friend of the best, most powerful, most famous person in the world. It can happen! *Jesus wants you to be his friend.* And he has arranged to meet you. That meeting is just one prayer away!

****

Bible Verses:

"God accepted Abraham because he believed. So his faith made him right with God." And that's not all. God called Abraham his friend. --James 2:23

Once we were God's enemies. But we have been <u>brought back to him</u> because his Son has died for us. Now that God has brought us back, we are even more secure. We know that we will be saved because Christ lives. ¹¹ And that is not all. We are full of joy in God because of our Lord Jesus Christ. Because of him, God has brought us back to himself. --Romans 5:10-11

"I am the vine. You are the branches. If you remain joined to me, and I to you, you will bear a lot of fruit. You can't do anything without me." -- John 15:5

"No one has greater love than the one who gives their life for their friends. ¹⁴ You are my <u>friends</u> if you do what I command. ¹⁵ I do not call you slaves anymore. Slaves do not know their master's business. Instead, I have called you <u>friends</u>. I have told you everything I learned from my Father." --John 15:13-15

Even though you have not seen him, you love him. Though you do not see him now, you believe in him. You are filled with a glorious joy that can't be put into words. --1 Peter 1:8

Reflect Questions:

1. Why did God decide to call Abraham his friend? What was Abraham's relationship with God before he believed? What do you think friendship with God really meant for Abraham (James 2:23)?

2. If we are not God's friends, what are we? How do we get from being far from God to being back in his good graces? What is the result of our being "brought back to God" (Romans 5:9-11)?

3. How close is a branch to the main stem it grows out of? What is the value of such a vital attachment? What happens if a branch is cut off from the main stem? What is Jesus' point (John 15:5)?

4. Who comes to mind when you think about someone who gives their life for a friend? Why does Jesus call his followers friends? If Jesus were your friend, what might that look like (John 15:13-15)?

5. Is it possible to be the friend of someone you've never met? Do you think it's possible to have a friendship with Jesus, even if you have never seen him (1 Peter 1:8)?

Step-of-Faith Prayer

Dear Jesus. I am amazed that you want me as your friend. I am even more astonished that you died on the cross to make that possible. I ask you now to forgive all my sin so that I can be right with God and become your friend forever. I accept your offer of salvation. Though I can't see you, I know that you are there and that you know me. I know that you will keep your promise to save me. Thank you! I rejoice that you will be my friend forever. I hope to be a "branch" that bears much fruit. Amen.

Group Share Time:

Who are some of your best friends? What have they meant to you? How have they affected your life?

Can you imagine having Jesus as a best friend? Have you ever thought about whether that is possible?

How do you react to the idea that Jesus wants this kind of relationship with you?

Word Meanings:

James 2:23 *Abraham* -- The founding father of the nation of Israel. He lived a life of faith and obedience and was called the "friend of God" (2 Chronicles 20:7).

James 2:23 *faith* -- To have faith is to believe. It is to know in your heart that God exists and trust that he will keep his promise to make you right with himself if you ask him to do so.

James 2:23 *made him right with God* -- Abraham became a friend of God.

Romans 5:10 *were God's enemies* -- Our sin separated us from God and put us in a state of hostility with him.

Romans 5:10 *brought back to him* -- Brought us back into a joyful, friend-to-friend love relationship with God. All wrongs were erased.

Romans 5:10 *will be saved* -- We will not come under God's wrath on judgment day.

John 15:5 *"I am the vine"* -- Jesus is the source of all spiritual life.

John 15:5 *"you are the branches"* -- You need to be attached to Christ to receive the life he gives.

John 15:14 *"You are my friends"* – Christ knows you well and loves you.

John 15:15 *"not. . .slaves"* -- We serve God not because we are forced to but out of love and gratitude.

APPENDIX E

Next Steps

If you have taken the step of faith, then you have taken the first and most important step a person can ever take--the beginning of your faith journey. Congratulations! Now you will want to think about the next steps. Most believers have found the following five practices to be vital steps in their faith journey.

1st Develop a Bible Reading Habit

There are many good reasons to read the Bible. The Bible teaches us what is true about God, about ourselves, and about our world. It gives us accurate information about the unseen world of angels, demons, heaven, hell, and life after death. It sheds light on practical topics like love, money, sex, friendship, work, and marriage. It can keep us from making umpteen mistakes. It's a rare treasure. But it has value only to those who read it regularly and come to know it well.

The Importance of the Bible:

God has breathed life into all Scripture [the Bible]. *It is useful for teaching us what is true. It is useful for correcting our mistakes. It is useful for making our lives whole again. It is useful for training us to do what is right. By using Scripture, the servant of God can be completely prepared to do every good thing.* --2 Timothy 3:16-17

Recommended Bible Readings:
- An all-time favorite psalm -- Psalm 23
- The life and ministry of Jesus – the Gospel of John
- Jesus' Sermon on the Mount -- Matthew 5-7
- How sin was vanquished by Christ and the Spirit -- Romans 8

2nd Pray Regularly

Prayer is the conversational part of your new love relationship with the Father and with Jesus Christ. It's the best possible way to grow in your relationship with them. By means of prayer, you can talk to the Father and the Son any time and anywhere. You can also hear them speak to you through the Word and the Spirit. In other words, prayer is a two-way conversation. The Father and Son love to converse with you.

The Importance of Prayer:

"This is how you should pray. 'Our Father in heaven, may your name be honored. May your kingdom come. May what you want to happen be done on earth as it is done in heaven. Give us today our daily bread. And forgive us our sins, just as we also have forgiven those who sin against us. Keep us from sinning when we are tempted. Save us from the evil one." --Matthew 6:9-13

Recommended Readings on and Practices of Prayer:

- Jesus' teachings on prayer -- Matthew 6:5-13; 7:7-12
- Paul's teaching on prayer -- 1 Timothy 2:1-4, Ephesians 6:18
- An acronym to recall the basic practices of prayer (ACTS):
  A - Adoration -- express love and admiration to God
  C - Confession -- acknowledge to God sorrow for sin's offenses
  T - Thanksgiving -- express gratitude to God for his gifts of love
  S - Supplication (intercession) -- claim the promises of God
     for yourself and for others

3rd Adopt a Christian Lifestyle of Love

The lifestyle you choose is critically important. It will affect your thinking, your actions, your values and your relationships. It will affect how you spend your time, your energies, and your money. A Christian lifestyle is basically a lifestyle of love. Choosing a lifestyle shaped by love for God and for others will make love the determinative factor in your life.

The Importance of a Lifestyle of Love:

One of the teachers of the law. . . asked him [Jesus], *"Which is the most important of all the commandments?" Jesus answered, "Here is the most important one. Moses said, 'Israel, listen to me. The Lord is our God. The Lord is one. Love the Lord your God with all your heart and with all your soul. Love him with all your mind and with all your strength.' And here is the second one. 'Love your neighbor as you love yourself.' There is no commandment more important than these."* --Mark 12:28-31

Recommended Readings on Christian Lifestyle:

➢ The Ten Commandments -- Exodus 20:1-17
➢ The way of love -- John 13:34-35, 1 Corinthians 13:1-13
➢ Peter's teaching on lifestyle -- 2 Peter 1:5-8

4th Connect with Other Believers (Fellowship)

We all need friends. If you are a new believer you will especially want friends who are strong believers. You can best find these by getting plugged into a church or a small group with other Christians. There you can be loved, embraced and prayed for. There you will find warmth, friendship, and acceptance. That's the kind of place where you will grow spiritually.

The Importance of Fellowship:

Let us consider how we can stir up one another to love. Let us help one another to do good works. And let us not give up meeting together. Some are in the habit of doing this. Instead, let us encourage one another with words of hope. Let us do this even more as you see Christ's return approaching. --Hebrews 10:24-25

Recommended Readings on Christian Fellowship:
- ➤ The togetherness of the first-ever church -- Acts 2:42-47
- ➤ Devotion to one another -- Romans 12:10-16

5th Tell Others about Christ (Witnessing)

Let me encourage you to let others know of your newfound faith early on. There are so many people out there who do not know what it means to have a relationship with Jesus Christ. Some of them are your friends and acquaintances. Many of them will be eager to hear about your new relationship. You can share with them out of the freshness of your new love for Jesus in ways that will make them want what you have. Tell them how you came to know Jesus and how they too can have a relationship with him. The Christian church grew from its very beginning by the testimony of new believers who were excited about their newfound faith.

<u>What the Bible Says about Witnessing:</u>

"But you will receive power when the Holy Spirit comes on you. Then you will tell people about me in Jerusalem, and in all Judea and Samaria. And you will even tell other people about me from one end of the earth to the other". --Acts 1:8

So faith comes from hearing the message. And the message that is heard is the message about Christ. --Romans 10:17

<u>Recommended Readings on Witnessing:</u>

- ➢ Jesus calls his followers the "light of the world." -- Matthew 5:14-16
- ➢ Jesus tells about finding lost sheep. -- Luke 15:1-7
- ➢ Jesus makes a convert. -- Luke 19:1-9

www.ingramcontent.com/pod-product-compliance
Lightning Source LLC
Chambersburg PA
CBHW070550010526
44118CB00012B/1284